The Politics of

Poetry, by Kendra Muecke
Vol. I

केंद्र

The Politics of
Copyright © 2017 by Kendra Elisabeth Muecke
A New Age Wasteland Prod.
ALL RIGHTS RESERVED
content written 2008 - 2017
in Houston, TX - Malibu, CA
Venice Beach, CA - Denver, CO
ISBN 978-1-849-14696-8

www.thepoliticsofkendra.com
@Kenbunny

All rights reserved. This book or any portion thereof may not be reproduced or used in any manner whatsoever without the express written permission of the author, Kendra E. Muecke

*Poetry
in the spirit of dedication!*

Be The Wind...

table-of-contents

Book, Me 17
Mountainous Man 21
New Age Wasteland 23
Fluffy Bell Bottoms 31
Let There Be Words 32
Therefore, I Am 35
1/1/16 Freewrite 37
Watch Yourself, Learning 38
Parliamentary, Watson 39
The Flower 40
Rose & Park 41
The White Board 42
Sweet Orange, Deep Blue 43
Walk With Me [The Teacher & The Golden Girl] 46
Stranger Than Autobiography 49
Listen 49
Miss Texas 49
How Many Me's [Moose Howl] 50
The Autumn [Winter] Queen 52
Golden Girl Meets Rainbow Boy 56
The Mediumship [Tether The Sails] 58
Sleepy as Pancake 59
New Wage Caseland 60
The Politics of Peace 66
The Manipulation [Current, See!] 67
The Dislike 67
Goner 67
Number: January 3, 2009 68
Statement of a Toll 71
Civil / Rowdy 72
Work for Freedom (20 c / hr) 73
K I T M 74
Inspiration is The Theme of A Place 75
The Call Out 76
AAAA Hello 76
Wild Craze 76
One More Grave, I Am Done 77
Sentiments 77
Three Days to Blame 77
The New Somatic 77
Letters from Vietnam 78
Hide 79
I See It 80
To Live 80
Totemed Up Freestyle 81
Made in Same 83
Sims 84
The Close Out [Stay] 85
To Be Birds of a Feather 86

Through The Pinwheel 87
Words from Brother 90
Words from Higher Self 91
Portal - Able 92
Perspectivity: The Tale of The Queen & The Sad One 94
Words from Lover 96
Words from Sister 97
Oxen and Buffalo 98
A Strike 99
Silbury Hill 100
8/8/13 100
A Daisy & A Twig 101
The Weatherman [HAARP] 103
Mr. Right 104
Words from Friend 112
Words from Messenger 113
Oh, Tweeze! 114
She Came in Through The Broken Arrow 114
Love and Haight 114
Federal 115
Stoned Gold Fox: 115
5-Point Star 115
11:11 115
Possible Band Names 116
Bridge 6 118
The Ides of Joy 118
Songstress 118
Welcome, This is A Wheelhouse 119
The Ghost 120
Seven Sisters, One Pact. 122
Ode to Dancer 123
Spiritous — 124
Golden Chaos 124
Plato's Chair 125
Ode to Healer 125
The Sociology of Staring 126
Get Out of My Laboratory 126
| 127
Words from Chief 128
Words from Stranger 129
Impossibly [Louvre] 130
With Thee 132
Sunday, Mundane 132
Frosty 132
Eggs and Bacon 132
The Golden Dictionary (Ticket) 132
Pushing Flowers 133
Something Over Nothing: The Teenage Years 134
Act Pretty 136
Rotational Returns [Reach the Summit] 137
The Seal 138
Mountainous Girl [Love is Valleys] 140

Overheard 140
Degrade A Beef 141
Lying to Yourself: For Dummies 142
The Song 143
The Girl with the Tambourine 144
Interdimensional Fable 145
A Thinking Place 146
Melt 148
A Series of Self: Kendra, pt. I 152
Processing the Negatives 153
Whilst in The Fiction of Skeletal Measures: Sonnet I 154
¿Dónde Está Mí Cabeza? 155
Dead Fish 156
Will, Son! 157
The Dreamer's Lament 158
Mark of The Trade 159
Lady Justice: Wake Up in the Late Afternoon 160
A Series of Self: Kendra, pt. II 161
888 - 555 162
Sugaree 163
Summer 164
Butterflys* With Bandages 165
A Series of Self: Kendra, pt. III 166
A Series of Self: Kendra, pt. IV 167
Panorama's Box 168
Invocation of Soul, By Self 169
Jedi Mind Bricks [Jet Eye Mined Fix] 170
Smarter Than the Average Elephant 171
—Contort— 171
The Butterfly Effect 172
Good in the Hood 174
To Become The Word Processor ft. Kenbunny 174
Bertha 175
Stevie Windwood [Hand Me The Guitar] 175
The Lot 175
9 in a Bottle 176
What'd You Find 178
AĀBABEFĀBABGHĮCDČEFEAËFEGHÍ 178
Energy 178
Aquarius 179
Scheme Free Rise 179
The Portrait 179
8 on Tour, 11 on Shore 180
Fixed Sand 184
The Experiment 185
Tinker 186
Shamanic Witch 188
Medicinal Man 189
If 190
Flip My Switch 191
Antiquity 192
The Companion 193

Karmic Names 194
Channel 11, Parallel News 195
Tighten Up 196
Me vs. You vs. Me 198
Fact & Opinion vs. Advice 198
Mind's Maid Up 198
The Send Off 199
60409 200
Field Notes: Slanted Poetry, Tales of Drunken Sound 201
Western World 202
Manifest Destiny: Instant Manifestation Nation 203
Share Your Shoes 204
Reservation(s): 206
Live @ 207
Plato's Star 207
#ReGeneration 207
The Pulley 208
The Grateful Lovers 210
My Own [I'm Not There] 211
The Traveler's Diary 212
It is Windy Outside The City 212
The Devil's Advertisement 214
Illuminine (9), Not Undermine 215
October 216
Sign Language 218
The Chronicles of I Don't Care 219
The Lullaby of Lady Liberty, nyc. 220
The Formular 221
Johnny Boy 222
Aromatic 223
Transmutation 224
Around The Bodhi Tree, Verses of A Mirror 225
Encounters 226
Ж 227
Touch of 230
I See You [The College Essay] 232
The Salivation 234
Jams, pt. I 235
The Sun Greets The Moon 236
Thanksgiving Eve 2009 238
Pendulum 239
Trill 240
Adjacent to Black Top 242
Arpeggios 243
Ekphrastic 244
Ekphrastic, II. 245
Ekphrastic, III. 246
33333 247
Sugar 248
Stories 249
[Karmic] Jams, pt. II 250
Spoken Truism 252

5 253
Sigh bore, hack… 254
12/12/13 255
Tell Me About You 255
House, Keeping 255
The Synchronicity 256
New Age Wasteland: Papa… oh, really? 257
Mac & Wood 257
The Vision 257
Copper Gold 258
Next-pionage 260
Magna Carta 261
The City for Miles 262
A Peaceful Treaty 263
The Gill of 264
Flowerette 265
Sunny Stand 266
And Still 266
Relation5ship 267
Ears Up 267
Sweet Love 267
Who is He? 268
The Night Cap 269
The Power Grid 270
34 '09 15 Years 272
The Fourth Gospel 274
February 11 275
Diablo Blanco 275
Tears of Joy 276
Whoooo Are You? 278
Luma Sunset 280
Honey and Oatmeal 280
Mannequin 280
Optional 280
3:31 am 280
Phantom, pt. III 281
Forgive me, please !! 282
Moontribe 284
Degeneration Nation 285
Found Electricity 286
A Sheep in Wolf's Clothing 288
About Time 290
The Politics of You: Acting in Dimensional Alignment 291
Little Wings / Big Ticket 292
Raven 294
Loving Eyes 295
YAWP 296
Whatever It Takes [The Hymn] 298
Sugar Magnolia 298
Fun 298
The Stand-in Hotel 299
10/19/14 299

Comrade Down 299
Instrumental Breakdown 299
Puppet Act 300
23 301
The Dozing Dozen: ~~Contemplation~~ 302
Wailing Afternoon 303
Milton Ralston Brown [Grandfather Mountain] 305
We Are Farmers [A Dedication to The Browns] 307
League of Legends 309
Not 1% Sure 314
Souly Now 315
Words from Mother 316
Words from Father 317
Words from Self 318
A Series of Self: Kendra, pt. V 319
New Moon in Virgo 322
Buffalo Walk 324

Acknowledgements 329
Thank You 334
About The Author 335

thank you

I encourage you to see these words
as offerings;
chant me,
read me,
light a candle
and say
"how do ya do?"

Book, Me.

It starts with the shadows,
when you look around and see,
how it starts with seeing the glimmer
in an eye of another.
When it starts, you begin by picking up on the rhythm
of repeated sounds around you—
You start by wondering,
*What this huge existential crisis is
and why people call it "Life".*

Life? ——
What a jiff of a joke.
You mean I have to put on clothes everyday
and pick out some obscure emotion to wear?
Yes, go ahead and plaster it to your face—
Call it a smile, call it a smirk,
Call it a glass full of unresolved realizations;
Call it a book,
and repeat after me,
"Welcome to my life."

Cue the horns and enter the dancers;
it's showtime, and my tits of a secret are out on display—
Don't look! Don't touch! Just feel—
Feel it coursing through your veins—
The cynical bitch of me;
the girl who goes where many a thought have driven itself before—
to the brink of insanity.
Remain calm, we won't be jumping off the ledge on this tour,
but for the ride of a lifetime, consider bungie-jumping,
maybe grab a wingsuit,
maybe not.

Understandably, I found myself in quite a conundrum.
Oh, how do I open to the pages of my own book?
It's crafted in lunacy and trustful on each account,
yet what will everybody think of me?
I pondered each second, as I wondered on what idea to begin.
How can I stand on the shoreline of self-description
without becoming intoxicated
by the words of my own (self) belief?
How again could I stand in the presence of another
without falling like a snowflake onto the street?
How could I ever conjure up the spirit of inspiration
and do such a beauty justice?
How could I?
What was I thinking?
A story…?
A word for word detailed outline of exactly who I am
and for what faith in reality I stand…?

It had to be a river of conscious decision;
a river of courage that flowed from the crust
of my sandwiched bones to the glide of my teeth.
Brevity with the breath of wit.
Love with the contention of delusion desire.
Life without the legitimacy of death.
How could I tell a story so descript in its own depth that
the looming presence of a skull could only but revive?
How?
And where does She begin?

— — — —

She was walking down the halls of her first memory,
a lane filled with roses & daisies & sunflowers.
She was walking hand in hand with her father
down the street of her first residence.
She was asking her father sweet questions
in a talk only the two could hear.
She was too young to actually speak,
but her presence amplified her truthful voice even more.
Her first memory comes in flashes,
packaged up in the beginning of a beautiful anecdote
founded on the flame of reconciliation.

Her first memory begins as her father reaches up to get her ice-cream.
Her feet on the lush grass, her eyes gazing onto a sugary dream
of a bright orange popsicle that would certainly melt too soon
in the beauty of the Texas sun,
leaving with it a trace of a Summer smile that she wore proudly
like a ribbon for her hair.

She was born in Houston, Texas
in the year of (19)93.
She was born on a crisp morning
to a mother who could also dream.
She arrived on cue, as she will always.
She arrived with peach fuzz
to a mother who was smiling.
Her name she could speak to you,
but she feels so absurd for doing—
For who cares about Alice in her own wonderland?
A pack of cards, who tells her to play the Ace on each demand?
— — — — — — — — — —

In the beginning,
there was a man,
moving swiftly;
left to right,
foot by foot,
edging up to the summit
of inner,
in her heart.

Life is a paradoxical state of mind— A state, in which, one can simultaneously experience a sense of inner-connectedness and communion with others, while also, experiencing a sense of solitude through the natural separation of matter into specific physical forms. By recognizing our duality within our multiplicity, we establish a society of consciously-connected human beings, who are aware of their power and justly moving.

Why do I accept mediocrity when I could have boundless happiness?

Flowing forth from all mediums of aesthetic self-expression, art creates infinite methods of learning about one's self. Through the proper channeling and usage of our unique and divine experience, humans can bridge the gap of misunderstanding that lies between one's earth-bound ego and one's everlasting soul. By learning about ourselves through art, we detach from the correlated perspective at hand and create a sense of dualism from the vantage point of singularity; this allows space for humanity to question our opinion of what defines a living, breathing, active society; for me, it's a society that encourages the honest vocalization of each person's inner truth, as well as, the practice and creation of new sacred traditions through actions, words, and shared interpretation. *Through the symmetry in the mirror to the contrast in a view, seeing our differences as our likenesses brings about a relative thought—*

And now, the rant :

Some of humanity's current truths may be hard to confront, but this is why we, as a people, must look at *both* our shared fears and our personal fears.

We must redefine our concept of words and communication at large, for words are the coordinators of symbolistic (symbolic) expression and vice versa; therefore, when studying historical specifics, the crux of seeing our current events as a reflection of our actions becomes a pivotal point of observation.

At which point does an idea begin to crumble: when an initial fear or threat is discovered, or when the laziness sets in?
Furthermore, what is laziness, but a broad term used to blanket our doubt?

During a time characterized by the worldwide ability to constantly communicate with one another at any hour of the day, we must question the actual status and appearance of humankind's ever-shared
and ever-changing **reality.**

Through identification and personalization of our dreams, breakthroughs, and habits, we can root the ideas that serve us, while also, ridding ourselves of those ideas that do not serve us any longer.

To see ourselves home and rediscover our faithful footsteps, we must accept all of our reflections— [as we manifest ourselves into the flow of daily patterns connecting the reality of our lives]. Drawing forth from our understanding of reason and rationality, these observed patterns require a consistent (constant) source of mental, physical, and spiritual energy in order to remain in the realm of existence.

Through our physical bodies, we can choose to live for joy or to live for fear; as a mode of evolutionary transition and development, we must learn to identify, but not judge, the inner voice of each moment. We must tune our ears to hear our *deepest* rhythm— the rhythm that fills every single moment, echoing sweet divinity through the perfectly detailed adjustment and on-going maintenance present in the inevitably - changing face of now.

If we can agree that our overall perception of reality pulses with change, yet still seems to remain stagnant— We can learn to identify the differences in an experience that causes our minds to label our existence as life vs. strife. Tracing our emotional memory back to its source, we can move closer into healing the cause of a mistake, instead of attempting to heal its symptoms.

May my mistakes forever fill me full of life and reveal the parallel between patterns vs. trends.

And now, I wonder how one puts theory into action?
In other words, what drives me?
[Diving deeper, what dreams me?]

In search of the truest vine of my soul, I dedicate this waking life to following my dreams—
but I have a lot of dreams…

So, in-order to fully grasp my soul's sole purpose, I break down the shapes of my thoughts, visions, and inspirations. By facing how I feel mentally, physically, and spiritually, I catch onto the emotional patterns of my personality—
a find of what pulls the heart.

To be, or not to be the whole that is myself? To be a conscious human-being: who chooses to walk the path of (righteous, radical, and personal) self-expression, who chooses to reside in the presence of now—
To be a living and breathing character of the book of life.

**I began finding the scattered pieces of myself,
once I allowed myself to be found.**

I had been wading in the comfort of my past. Knee-deep in anxiety with a head-full of far-out ideas, when I realized that the comfort I thought I had been feeling was not comfort, it was paralysis.

On the outskirts of social normality, about 11 blocks South of Main Street, I met weirdness in the form of the good 'ole grateful counterculture. Specifically drawn to the peace-packed hippy movement of the 1960's, I read about, *and I felt about:* racial justice, political justice, and the justice of good vibes— that seemed to be right around any corner.

However, let us look at where our species wades now.

Under the weight of unnecessary, unexplained, and unceasing times of war, some may forget to ask, "Where is the world peace?"

**So, I will speak for crowd and ask, "Where is the world peace,
and why can't we share it with one another?"**

I want an actual answer, not this over-cooked gumbo of shits and giggles served with a side of bread and circuses. I want an answer. I want a debate. I want to live in a world that does not allow its inhabitants to murder each other over oil and opium. Playing the great game of tug o' war over the ego waffles of their balanced breakfasts—
leggo my ego [*check if 'leggo' is TM] . Yeah, shit really escalates quickly—
when a writer starts thinking… or *stops*.
Damn, beats me.

Oh, and of course, there is democracy, the bread and butter of the West… Well, look, I'm not Hunter S.— Yes, but my penny for a thought gives everyone this proposition:
Why do we support the current war? *What war?*
Are we that scared of communicating? *Am I?*
Are we really too scared to sit down in a room, hire some translators,
and discuss the validity of any reason to this negative rhyme? *Huh?*

Stand up for peace, **or don't**… I will regardless. I will gladly stand, sit, pace around, and listen to anyone who thinks they have an argument that justifies the use of violence to gain power. I will sit and objectively listen to all who wish to continue living in this age of fear, but I don't think the debate would get anywhere. We would see the stupidity in our passive decisions and agree to never act so silly again.

On the bright side, it makes me happy to see so many people contributing and working to regenerate the current definition of sustainable permanence. Through starting conversations about the nature of true cultural growth, we can begin to ripple out in hopes our generation will put down the phone, pick up a pencil, and start writing our own history, a history of the cultivation of communication
[and how all these different routes of communication have the potential to further cultivate our society or destroy it].

Throughout the entire globe, the question facing our current civilization is not,
"When will we find the right leader?", it is,
"When will we become our own leaders?"

It is easy to plant seeds— It is easy to share our opinions, post tweets about #worldpeace, and lounge in the security of living in a society that makes all of our decisions for us.

The hard part is taking responsibility for the seeds you don't water.

**We shall continue moving forward,
while still keeping our previously planted seeds in mind—
Trusting our soul's intuition to grow in the directions that call to our hearts— The directions that walk us home.**

An abstract of sorts:
New Age Wasteland (Productions) is an all-inclusive, all-immersive, aesthetic alliance of alternative artistic expression. Positively, founded on the beauty of essence and the essence of truth. It is a collective of voices, reflecting art back onto itself.

Branding together in shared reason, shall we stand up for our public airwaves?

So, we question:
How can we level the worldwide economic playing field?
How can we view our own self-worth as more valuable than money? Together could we create art: music, television shows, films, novels, etc. that serve a larger purpose and a larger population? Could society use (artistic) self-expression to surpass all false misconceptions? Could we collectively create a consciousness that values worth over wealth and character over class?

<u>New Age Wasteland</u> is an agreement to aim past your tide's reach.

Envisioning the tide of the 1960's, we see the dream of a classless counterculture remains, for it's a hand-me-down; (scattered, but not lost)— And as we search to find the high-water mark, where the thoughts finally broke and rolled back, we will find that peace had been waiting, patiently, inside the right kind of eyes. Through the power of performance art and the presence of written work, I want to discuss and share my experience of existence thus far. I am living for joy. I am living for peace.

The Mission: turning inner-knowing into outer-creation

— to take care of the plants we hoped would sprout from the dust, pushing light through the cracks in our stress, or to keep feeding our endless infatuation with that which disrupts and decays? To have peace or to have war? To remain in arrogance and ignorance, or to schedule a meeting to discuss the possibility of setting a date, inwhich, all humanity can agree to let one another be, peacefully? However, what is there really to agree on? What isn't there to agree on? Should we begin to reclaim the freedom we have never truly known? Or shall we continue to avoid all topics of importance? Where can we start to do something? Is there even anything to do— Will we even try? Will we even take the time to finish reading this comment? …

When will we realize that we have been treating green lights like they are yellow, turning yield signs into ones that make us *stop*— because we all make our own excuses, but when will we, *when will I*, realize that even escape is an illusion? Trying to avoid me, myself, is to be childish— It makes me like Wile E. Coyote chasing the Road Runner, failing day in and day out. Never re-examining my methods, never trying something new— always succumbing to conflict, using those cute-little cartoon ACME explosives, missiles, and weapons—You know, the one's that never work correctly. Those factory-faulty weapons that keep Wile E. Coyote in a constant chase, because either the coyote cannot figure out how to properly use the weapon, or because that is the nature of ACME's ethic:
to always keep the consumer in a state of consumption?

I have always wondered why the coyote even wanted to blow up the Road Runner, because, if the Road Runner was dead, then Wile E. Coyote would have no show left; the network would drop him. There would be no conflict to watch—
—this is true— Also, if he would have caught up the Road Runner, only to find out, *'he's kinda cool, I think we could be friends.'* The humor would be lost. However, children's cartoons point out how using violence and picking fights (with people you do not know and who are different than you are) is a never-ending battle. Like Wile E. Coyote, have we locked ourselves into a routine of confusing the attempted solution with the actual problem?

It is 2017, so I hear, and our civilization's ability to communicate with anyone, in anyplace, at anytime is at an all time high. The idea that our technological inventions have, apparently, superseded our *'oh, so simple, cute little human brains'*— is a lie; it is entirely false. We have just chosen to not use our rational thinking, nor use our heart. I am typing on a laptop right now— Think of how difficult it must have been to figure out how to put these little parts of parts of parts together, in-order to mould energy into form. It must have been more difficult than being a rocket-scientist performing brain surgery, and I know there are more comprehensive technological inventions out there, but that is my point.

What I am trying to say is, APPARENTLY, humans are smart as fuck. We can create things that, at one time, seemed impossible, yet, the only thing that no leader, no president, no corporation, no institution, and no person has been capable of creating is world peace on Earth. There must be something more to it, because it seems so simple. Desiring peace, seeking balance, nourishing one's hope and not one's despair— seems as innate and natural as breathing.
So, *let's breathe*, and let's chill out, before we spend all our money buying ACME products, only to come to see that we are fighting our own selves.

I will forever remember the 21st century as the era that we finally ended war.

The war on the war of the warring war on (insert catchy, provoking, distracting issue here). Critics are calling it the biggest prank of all time. See the movie everyone is trying not to talk about, a tale of misguided passion and disillusion. The Summer's most hilarious psychological thriller, winner of the *"We the People, By the People" Award.* This Summer, come see the movie that will have you wondering, "Is this a true story?"— *The War on War: Revenge of the Absent*— the sequel to last year's groundbreaking movie, *"The War on Debt: To Be the Silent Killer."* Coming soon to a theater near you. In other news, Hurricane Hurrytabuymore is approaching slowly, but surely, we are advising all viewers to prepare for an emergency situation. Prepare for looting, However, in the meantime. Please continue to buy as much as possible. Thanks for joining See-B.S. nightly blues, I'm Ashton Kutcher, stay punk'd America!
WE INTERRUPT THIS IMPORTANT PROGRAMMING SESSION
to test the disaster-delagating-disease and de-evolvement dollar menu special.
In other news: according to Dignifing-Diversity-Daily's latest December digest, ducks have stopped quacking this season— for fear of losing bread. Leader of local pond, Duck McFuckMe, has denounced himself a Dadaist, saying, "Dozens of disorientated daughters are disguised and done." Done dutifully in downtime, we all have to agree, here down at the station while digesting these double-double decker domesticated dingos during darkly dank destines of dying dreams— has been found to cause death and doting, donning, and dilation of the liver.

In sports, Wookies, *also known as Couch-walkers,* have announced they've retired. Apparently, once done downstairs, the Dead Heads destroyed the depth of infinite doors by downing downers whilst down around the dungeon. Boldy, 99% are said to be free of distinct and darkened doings, yet characterized by mood swings of de&reprogrammed-demons-in-dependence of decent and dictating-devilishdeplorements. It's deadening-degraded and now dehumanizing the American people's dinner tables. **ATTENTION !** We have just gotten word that today's Chief Weatherman has called in the directions sick. So, that's it for us here, because I am too white to give a damn about climate change.

Keep watching Fear & Groaning Channel 11 News—
drugging you up with discounted, damnanizing drama, that is guaranteed to conjure up even the lowest of spirits. Rinse, lather, and repeat. Take 1 pill in the morning with a complete balanced breakfast.

[click here to see the 7 must-have accessories this season. It's autumn— are you ready for THE fall?]

FLUFFY BELL-BOTTOMS

Major Arcana XIII: Death (2014), by Ericka Frost

kings become jokers,
when a hand is a hand,
dealt through dual recreation,
fatality lurks & casts shade forth on today's land,
without permission or regards to thy man,
shadows lead individuals to label by class
or to take a stand—

LET THERE BE WORDS
four score

The forest is calling,
and it is so,
the woods call often,
but I ignore the phone—

Technologically speaking,
& technically, in-fact,
I retrieve information from the source,
whether it is Wikipedia or exact—

I asked the butler a few times,
but he spilt the milk on me,
he may have been full of answers,
but was too busy crying.

Speaking out loud,
most tongues ring out of tune,
I assume, my anatomy book was not lying,
when it called The Bible out too.

For who would lie,
about the citation of their prophecy?
When there is concentration of awareness,
masses may fall ill to fallacy.

"Spread the Good News!"
I could bellow it for eternity—
From deep within my internal sun.

But I guess,
we all have better things to do,
than sit around,
and discuss where we are from.

For example, we could play a quick game of Life,
and then the winner could buy us all ice-cream,
or we could go on a jog,
while singing in perfect harmony!
___ ___ ___ ___

I'll call it a day,
I'm grateful for that,
My mind can now unravel,
and ripple out to contact.

SEAL OF THE LEAGUE

Do you remember?

Yes.

THEREFORE, I AM
The Summer Queen

What a novel idea to look into my eyes,
What a novel idea to walk circles in disguise—
What's a mirror filled with fog, when there's water to clear it?
What's a nose filled with breath that is needed to steer it?
How's the trace on my fingers going to hit you with hate?
What's the shame in a chewed word?
Lips say, "Participate"—
What's the ice of a comment without the liquid of a knight?
Why is language so complicated, cut with a silent knife?
What's the empty space behind a forehead have to do with choice?
What's the outline of a future have to do with voice?
Could the digits on my fingers be surrounding the clouds?
Could the outlook on my pastimes be concerning to those found?
Is the smoke from the fire invading your space?
Is the light from the sun exposing your true face?
How is the moon always rising, controlling the clock?
How are seconds always running without thoughts on lock?
When deceptions seek counters to stand on and dance,
I start to follow Alice into a certain trance.
Where's the hat filled with possible names?
Where's the life in a child who just sought a group of frame?
Is the independence on your tongue licking up my goodbyes?
Are the lashes on your sight correcting unjust eyes?
Do the palms on your hand tend to map out a certain fate?
Do I always come up for air in a blank, splattered state?
Should I stand for a mouth that gets fed broiled words?
Should I sit and just wait for my own slice of the world?
Because the blinker on your shoulder is growing ever closer,
And the femur on my knee is the newfound composer,
And the glory you painted and stapled to my face,
Is stepping towards the balcony and reaching out to play,
And the phrases from my head have grown little legs,
Surrounded by corruption crawling from underneath your bed.
And the path of the natives is reserved for certain feet,
And the wrath of one fruit is all I have to eat,
And the diamond on your backbone is glowing in the shade,
And I stand here and whisper your insanity to be made.

As the wind carries your cries from deep within my tomb,
Could dawn be worth a simple try, while my metal fingers cut up doom?
Is it crazy to sing and harmonize with shadows?
Is it strange to bellow yawps from distal golden gallows?
Do you see the solid conquerors dressed as a hatter?
Or is it only my mind that has discovered and tackled matter?
Who is the creator of a speech I attempt to speak?
Who is the demonstrator of a river I cannot seek?
Does time matter, as I construct these thoughts deep within your head?
Is it simple logic to cooperate with those once deemed dead?
Are you frightened at the thinkers that can think within this room?
Are you intimidated by the possibilities you embraced by chasing day out of Mother Nature's womb?
Is it embarrassing to mold letters from the ink of my hand?
Is it wrong to walk on afternoon's ground without sculpting a plan?
Are questions multiplying, as you long to be modest?
Are letters filled with Novembers meant to make the villain be honest?
Is the end a mentionable substance, clear to all who dream?
Is the final day a simple handshake, as the youth grips Winter's scream?
Could the membrane of your smile be all I have to see?
Is the thought process in my mind all I need, to **'be'**?
Can we say we are truly living the life placed in our hand?
There are words in my head.
Therefore, I am.

1/1/16 Freewrite
Repeat after me

Once and again, I hear a story that truly resounds within the depths of my hearing.
    Like shackles unbroken, I feel open
        when a community enjoys sharing about one's day, one's dress, or silly thoughts
            — *Communion for Communication, I find I've always sought.*

So, I bellow freely at times, opening up my chords to those who accept me and help me
    project collective happiness on the world—

        The false conception of destruction being an inevitable force
            tickles my existence and cinches certain nerves—
        To find purpose within context of plot is what I see,
            for if [when] I seek it, it's further from syncing.

With the limitations being none and the justice being bearable,
I look forward to new years that echo divine variables—
I am that which I am. This is true,
and I feel loving to my soul.

        To be wide awake is beautiful,
           and to be counted,
              equals one.

        Creation comes up next in the timeline of my head—
    How to shape with conviction and to let the light of Joy conquer.
Colors of winds I breathe — in my sleep — remind me of moments diving deep.

        To be Artsy and Fartsy is all it is chalked up to seem—
    Just remember to capture the presumptuous Golden Mean.

I am the Blooming Flower—
I am the Violet Flame—
I love Myself—
I love My Name—-

[time: 10 min]

WATCH YOURSELF, LEARNING

There is much more in play,
than a villain or a beast.
There is much more psyche,
in a resolution than in a theme.

PARLIMENTARY, WATSON

I
think,
I thought,
I remembered yet,
but quickly,
quite soon,
Well, I just… simply forget.

Whilst mid-saunter,
You see,
I rambled on through,
The dusk, quintessential, to forsaking the truth.

However, consequential sayings often miss the lot,
and writers, quite good, often leave out the plot.

It may be existential to remorse for being,
or it may be essential to seeing
and breathing.
I may have found a name for the person within me,
but I forgot, excuse me, please.

the flower.

       Divided creeds——

I'm balanced,

losing all I heed.

By the grace above me,

    I learn my foot takes lead.

                                    In the late night morning,

                                    when I could not find my way,

                                    the light turned on within me,

                                    ——much to my dismay.

                Bounce,
                  Float,
                 Elevate.

             Feathers form
             my backbone,
            Taking the path,
           I choose to create.

*   I am full of _____,*
           fill in the blank.

rose & park.

When I lose my wording

Where do I go?

    Do I break at the formation of a wave,

        Or do I continue to trace circles around my faith?

            About a person,

                Who is myself,

                    About a motif

                That delays itself—

    Til the tiller echoes from its grandstand

That America's beauty is ready to land.

THE WHITE BOARD

Chase many rabbits, catch one.

SWEET ORANGE, DEEP BLUE

Parallel, as if I am Eleven.

In thy chambers,

I peer amidst constructive meaning,

I care for those lost,

I care for those deceiving.

I walk in dignity,

& this is so.

— "on forth to the rhythm!" yells the salmon below.

To move, I beckon from the depths of my soul,

as if I needed words in my ear to behold—

To groove right by,

to shift & to mould,

to make everyday sunny—

as if you care what garbage I am told.

& shadows, & shadows, & shadows—
I see,
succulently dousing my spirit in false integrity.
To have found Waldo without even owning the book!!!

Oh, but of course! Quite normal you see—
I found him out back,
sauntering to the beat
of a drummer boy,
who owned nothing to eat.

So—
Proposing a question,

Where do all the manners of answered time go?

I think I left them outback– tied up like a stripper to the north pole.

Put on your
thinking cap,

Dig
on in,

Breathe
inside,

& Beheld
within.

Time to reap what I sow,

& to turn against boulders,

to see if they are real

or just calculated mental patterns.

[July 16, 2015]
7.16.15

Walk With Me [The Teacher & The Golden Girl]

The Teacher & The Student walk in from stage left, we join them in an ongoing conversation. As they are speaking, lights come up, following them to their destination. Upon arrival, the lights reveal their location as a street corner at a 4-way stop. When they arrive, it is on the upstage right street corner.

TEACHER
… Therefore, the conversation continues. It revels in our idea of bones,
and it picks our teeth up off the floor, as we are flabbergasted to find ourselves—

They come to a stop on upstage right street corner.

STUDENT
—back.

TEACHER
Right back where we began, on the precipice of decision.

STUDENT
… and arriving, we come to find the condensation of laughter
appears much lighter this time around.

TEACHER
For doubt no longer has a hand in your game of cards.

STUDENT
and no longer, do I see shadows around your eyes.

TEACHER
and no longer, are we stuck behind a foray of disguise.

STUDENT
Doubt. (scoffs)
I can't believe it got to me, at first…
I mean, I shook it off pretty well.

TEACHER
What? After all the back-tracking and
asking your peers for their opinion of you?

STUDENT
Well, yeah, I mean I just wanted to know that I was right
about what was right in-front of me…

TEACHER
and how did your need for validation appear for you?

STUDENT
My need for validation appeared to me like this street-corner, meeting in the middle in 4 ways, shaded in with the opaque concept of circumstantial surroundings. Myself, slowly revealing to me, in patterns, my state of karmic denial. It started by taking the form of lack of decision, lack of drive, lack of joy, showing up for me in the most tangible angst of self-suppression, like an artist turned bird in a cage… Then, I flew out of the nest of insanity, only to get swept up by a self-created fallacy known to me as— Writer's Block — I stood on this street corner, and I thought… Shit! I haven't anywhere to go! I haven't anything to do! Let alone someone to do it with! I have nothing, and so I was nothing. I was a devalued charade of my own personality, waiting behind the curtain of reality for some magician to pull my bunny ears out the hat of future pretense. I acted as if I were not the conductor of my own symphony, as if the light at the end of the tunnel was not the solitary moon hanging high in the sky. I acted as if I needed someone else to tell me who I was. So, I felt unsuccessful on all fronts, because I was glued behind the curb, not seeing myself in the reflection of the storefront beside me, not seeing my eyes gazing back at me from the puddle on the street, not hearing the truth in my own words, and so, I spent my time hanging my head in depression, the depression of stagnation, and I kept standing here, in silence, imagining cars whizzing by, nipping at my toes and feeding false recognitions of fear. I didn't want to leave the street corner, but I didn't want to stay either. I remember wanting to cross the street one day, from here across 11th Avenue to the otherside… It took everything in me to do it.

TEACHER
and now, you know what that everything means to you.

STUDENT
oh, mos def!

CUT TO:
The Student, also known as Golden Girl, is on a TV spot for Fear & Groaning, Channel 11 News. She is being interviewed by a representation of the ignorant source that is mainstream media.

INTERVIEWER
So, [Golden Girl]… Your most recent play, "Writer's Block" has been getting a lot of coverage. Many speculate the reasoning behind the relation of your quote on quote "writer's block" to a street corner. Does feminism have any backing for this sociological stand against the degradation of women?

GOLDEN GIRL
What?

INTERVIEWER
In your first scene, you are standing on a street corner, relating all your doubts to… standing on a street corner. What does that mean to you?

GOLDEN GIRL
Exactly the metaphor I used it for.
It appears as one thing, however,
'tis quite the relative opposite.

SCENE

STRANGER THAN AUTOBIOGRAPHY

To open up,
And listen to points,
That pull on my heart strings,
in lessons of choice.
To see the teacher in every smile,
To know I am the only one feeding on self-breed denial.
To realize I'm capsizing the boat in me.
I start over,
so I will only write sweetly.

LISTEN

Speaking with you
would be trust though—
I could see through
the illusions,
yet still respect
reflections known.

"In past," sights Approval
for my Upstanding Presence
and my Persistent Renewal.

For I love from
the depth of all shown;
I love the dove of
Grace,
When you play your
Guitar in that particular tone.

MISS TEXAS

Don't let the fear of striking out
Keep you from swinging—
Don't let the fear of Life
Keep you from living.

Somewhere, I guess. That's where I must begin.

HOW MANY ME'S [MOOSE HOWL]

It starts with the shadows,
and the resizing that all is resemblement
of earlier moments,
recast and informant.

I sing out loud,
and ask in answers;
How can I be more than a chance of "Her"?

And What's life got to do?
But shine and sun on til tomorrow.
What's love got to do?
Form a shape and then follow.

Follow me into the grass,
I saw a moose who said, "Alas!"
"The way is clear,
and the park is full
of whispers destined
upon the soil."

And filled the trunk to have a list,
And filled the funk to meld in mist,
To delve in deep
and never I miss,
The targeted individual
in fame for this.

The succulent sap
is blood running my marrow.
My raven passes by
looking and spawning
for the lift that brings the sparrow.

And found is the lost that speaks to me,
Through grounded renditions
of melodic aspen trees.

Who to be — ?
Who to last — ?
Far is the trek
that jinks the mast.

Who cracked the dawn
with the ray of face,
and made a
houndstooth undone
to the falsity
of race.

Lope away,
—lope, lope
destined into the distant.
I can see you in moments
that are reminiscent.

So,
I move —
And move —
And move on in —
I turn on
and turn out
And then I begin.

THE AUTUMN [WINTER] QUEEN

Creation of space,

Creation of sound,

Creation of who,

Creation of now,

Relation to me,

the birds see how.

Look into the eyes

of a forgotten frown.

Welcome to Pleasantview,

Welcome to noise,

Step into followship,

Step into ploys.

Reverse the signs,

Sign the reverse.

Green mellowed lies—

you leave on verse.

Spell the name,

Sound out the words,

Hold in your hands,

the center of my worlds.

Become a statue,

released from my shelf.

Whisper followed absence,

and watch us excel.

We engulf presence into art,

and life into being—

We see hovering condition,

Rainbow Braids,

Weaving—

Compute my circumstances,

and turn to my page,

Read all the credentials,

and force love out its cage.

Lock us in with your stare

of thy Holy perception,

Throw away the key,

I threw away deception.

Walk past my feet,

and set leaves

to be wed—

Trot past my mind,

and put stars in my head.

Fill my glass

with communal blessings

and watch trust conspire >>

into motion,

as belief,

becomes fire.

— Fluctuate —

and become a thing.

— Coordinate —

and fool the king:

"Stand up straight!

Lift your neck, your voice!

Retaliate spots!

Elbow the choice!"

Slightly pull on your lash,

and turn towards my face.

Kick my feet,

Pull me from my space.

Ask questions,

View name,

Shake heads at

coping with same.

———

View points,

View me,

View changing

—everything—

Open romantic eyes,

to the divine art of

wooooooooooooing.

January 13, 2009

GOLDEN GIRL MEETS RAINBOW BOY

There is a sounding on the wind
That catches lightness in its grin
And echoes fellowship
around
the gathered
Rumblings.

It's the movement
Of the West,
Towards Eastern dreams
once laid to rest.

Understood that OPEN FIELDS
plant seeds for GATHERING.

Turning to the page,
Where syllables come out to play,
Filling,
Breathing,
Lungs as shipments for receiving.

Informative notions of
a stone
That projects its history of
land all known.

from where >> **to be** >> **to go** >> **to face** >>
a mind
free
of chatter.

Holding numbers
on a phone
that cannot dial home.

We question trust,
but never
doubt
the latter.

To be taut
And made of brick,
A house not seeking
improvement.

— We then Transform,

       for Change is

       Predictable

       Rearrangement.

They told me to lead the way
*   — California*

THE MEDIUMSHIP [TETHER THE SAILS]

Psychic revealing becoming true,

Red joins green and sails on through,

Found to be the 1 in 3,

Upon the river,

A balloon floating:

Where's the meaning?

I ask out loud—

Why am I frightened out of being found?

When I see the set within the poster,

Do I edge on in and drift away closer?

Does the shore catch the beat

With the bait in hand

With a hook

To return to walking on land?

And flopping on my belly

Like a beast—

I tip off my mask

And let it see me.

Arise to meet those risen.

SLEEPY AS PANCAKE

Geometric are the angles
that coordinate the
cheese of said mind.
I prance along closer,
but have forgotten my next line—

It was an uncertainty

within the age of reason.

It was me against myself,

if advancement meant treason.

I was then
and am now,
Picking up the memories
by the hour;
A transition from haze,
something to do
with reclaiming one's power.

But, with much Ado,
"Your character and substance,"
give us all that we need—

They wanted ego to subside,
but they're the ones who brought back the 90's.

I stomp;
I step.
I'm on my own to unravel,
at the end of the day,
I remain the one
who experiences my travel.

New Wage Caseland

What is this gravity I am thinking and breathing?
Why do shadows cast themselves on those [who are] believing?
Receiving is one thing,
but telling is yet—
Blow the whistle on a revolution?
You'll certainly lose the bet!

I'm not trying to make enemies,
Well, maybe a few friends…
Just a group of buddies,
who are down to pretend!

———

Who are down
to drop out
of being commercial,
and admit
that breakfast
is a huge part
of being eternal!

So,
Why do we allow time to
put our eggs
into an afternoon scramble,
Sunny side up,
then,
it's the game of Life
without the manual.

———

My idea of fair
is not allowing
a dictionary
to be used
during Scrabble.
I tread on nothing
when I listen
on repeat
to The Rabble.

However,
The intention speaks up anyway…
Echoing words,
as it follows behind…

———

"Whatever! Whatever!
I am speaking my mind !!"

———

… Well, writing, of course,
but,
that's two of a kind,
and there's only one spot available
in the dark force
that is dined.

It's actually quite light,
but that's the irony,
you see,
you must enter the opaque
to genuinely succeed—

Because Earth moves round,
I've heard,
it's fast.
Would you consider
that gossip
or would you consider that fact?

———

When vultures swim laps?

I don't know, I don't care—

When I chill and relax.

———

Because the grass
is cool
and on both sides,
remain
a full glass.

… But casting the weather,
can be daunting in-fact,
mispredicting my appetite
is quite
deceivingly flat.

Why point a bowed arrow
at a target, you see?
I am confused about
systematic consumption
that is not
eating and drinking.

Roots grow deep—
Say a lot of cliches…
I get pissed about mainstream things,
yet,
Here I am,
Bitching away!

Philosophically:
Is action involved
in all plots
and tracks?

I keep asking question
after question,
I need to just
— like I said —
fucking relax!

But, wait!
My mind is racing,
but against who said?

      I don't know, nor care—

and end up fighting some mirror
until my dreams return **lucid.**

I'm sure it's fine,
It's just me
with thoughts on my mind,
and me with no shame
in the name,
as I drag out
each moment,
through the muddy depths
of collective brain.

Slow down the tempo—
I'd like to catch up.
"Where are we going?
Why did we even coin the word *corrupt*?"

What if I said
I could see marbles
falling straight
out my ears?
Would you be interested
in iridescent understanding,
like how age
is a miscalculation
of years?

Yes,
I know
how I sound…

But I get so stressed.

        I must be.

Be
who I am
or I'll cease
ceaselessly
to exist.

Cognizant,
I know.
I apologize,
This is true—
I'm just trying
to gain
Brownie points—
for Mother Earth
and Her crew…

Our World,
deep breath…
If we want to elegantly last—
I believe in a purposeful beginning—
and not a self-crippling
failed attempt
at a past.

It's decades now
That we've seen the view—
differential perspectives
within the same truth.

The same certainty,
The same bounce.

The same pep in my step.

The energy I need—
What we all can confess.

But, *Hey!*
Shit!
Don't shoot the messenger!
I'm just spouting
my mouth off,
since I'm always the worst passenger.

Clever rhymes are cute,
as we play in the youthful fountain!
"There's a source at the top
of this sparkly, snowcapped mountain !!"
———

And it's flowing - out - if that even makes sense—
…whatever metaphors…
You must know it exists!
The Rock of the Roll,
The Bread and the Butter,
I proclaim from the peak
about the mighty rhythm of another.

Turn off,
Tune out,
and
Drop in.

See y'all there!

I'm teasing you!

I double dare.

The Politics of Peace

We are not a lifestyle,

We are a society.

The Manipulation [current, see!]

Drift to a perception,
shut from the Earth,
where only uncommon sense
holds monetary worth.
        Frankly,
           I held the truth in my knuckles
           Then in my heels,
           I thought they had buckled, but
           no…
'twas the wind
yelling from
inside my ear.
      "That is only what you know.
      …so just drop it, dear."

The Dislike

People only hate one another
to feel a range of things.
We all secretly love one another,
confirming & inhabiting our reality.

Goner

Human emotions are not clean cut,
and his awareness of distance has become obstruct—
But what is desire in a world full of the compulsion to approach?
On the grounds of reciprocating, he is filling bunnies full of hope.
Loathing under trees that deserve nothing
but those who know to loafe,
She is full of intentions
but keeps rebuilding past ghosts.

Accept what is,
& what is will accept you.

NUMBER: JANUARY 3, 2009

Fleeting acceptance,

make me your witness,

force me close

with the arms atop your eyes.

Correct my mould

with the fingers from the sky.

Reverse my order,

and "Repeat machine."

Look in my eyes,

my mouth becomes mean.

Atop the surface of a Holy little hymn,

Atop the Earth,

I join the corps of men.

Is it the corps or corpse

dangling high above?

Is it rolling and shooting,

reaching to be loved?

Is it the cry outside your window,

as we learn to progress?

Is it the silver in my chair,

as I lay my head to rest?

Create a reason…

My thirty lost its four,

Commit to treason:

The promises to hold open the door—

But look!

As I am shattered

all along the hall,

the words are casting,

and I wait for my call.

I use cotton

to loosen

the jaw of my mouth.

I paint pictures of my voice,

and seek those who develop.

To hold the choice

of the head of the line,

To witness the riot—

It's the menace

soaking up time.

Through the pages,
let's try it,
and breathe it.
— shall we shake hands,
with the sane,
to linger

and defeat it?

STATEMENT OF A TOLL

Hear Ye! Hear Ye!
Get our hearing here!
Join the crowd
Of seldom done reassuring
and life left without billing
The found!

Hear ye, Hear ye!
Her license profound,
To gander the geese,
and honor the crown!

"Beware!" she says,
"The causation is creating a future for you!
A suture of camaraderie
composed of homelands a skew.
There's a building to scale
and a wall of few,
Who stand bland
and contrite
and full of blocking the truth."

"Their pants are high
and their ears are low!
They kid about a war
of which your wishing
wishes not to know!"
And in your sight,
You feel the sun.
You feel yourself
laughing out loud for fun.
The whole of your being
is the swing on your feet
that guides the spirit
to hold a soundful greet!
The way of your vibe
is the dig of your bone
founding the relation
and opulence *of perpetual tone.*

are you, real you?

"Civil engineer?
Nah, I'm a rowdy engineer"—

                                                                        "but sir,
                                                    it says right here on your card."

Work for Freedom (20 c / hr)

Where does the word *Merchant* go

to buy the phrases

used in common time.

        I asked for 7,

            they gave me 9—

To be bound backwards

and unraveling

offline.

Karma ain't got no devils
but the self you impose.

KITM

I repeat from self

unveiling

to yuhhhhhh.

— *This is true.* —

Luckily,

Just another

keg in the machine.

Inspiration is the theme of a place

Like regional whiteness
Taking in stride
its exceeding value
of monetary incentive.
Maximum to the touch
and quite out of sort,
Comes about the idea to destroy war.

We are here to drink beer.
We are here to kill war.

THE CALL OUT

Trap yourself in a box,
with no lid
and no surroundings.

Create a mind,
Intricate with locks,
And dance through fields with understandings.

Stop by the sign
With two arrows intertwined,
Become a being
Seasoned with thyme.

Reminisce on the hours spent
nuzzled up on the grass.
Remember, Remember,
The memories that were built to last.

AAAA HELLO

Reverse the signs,
Sign the reverse,
but tell me the truth!
The 'truth' was just sold.

WILD CRAZE

My favorite thing about
talking to myself
is not listening.

To be so inspired by everything,
that by the end of the day it's
uninspiring.
In-fact, it's like American Beauty—
Look at the bag floating in the wind...
... Ever seen anything like that?

What's words back
backwards...

ONE MORE GRAVE, I AM DONE

The fool is me;
It is not you.
I promised to stay selfish;
It was the only promise I followed all the way through.

I self-prophesied to be much at an age so little.
I would slowly carve away the stone,
because a shallow-soul is not one of a quitter.

I litter my peers with concern,
and I sprinkle them with disaster.
I wanted to be great,
but I turned out quite the latter.

SENTIMENTS

Don't be whom you once loathed.

THREE DAYS TO BLAME

Things are getting weird,
I will be just fine.

One day, one hour,
Each minute,
At a time.

THE NEW SOMATIC

Losing the notions we knew to keep,
Dying to draw a tie between crime and peace.
Through sound, we arrived at a gathering of several, or nine.
Sectored into distinctions, we saw that regeneration would take time.

I'd like to get you drunk.

Letters from Vietnam

Rivers flowing wide,
Across my state of mind,
Perceptions holding distance,
A laden ship with no captain.

Retreat! Reverse! Fall on me!
Lakes close to rivers,
Rivers summon the creek.
"Fall down! Fall down!"
They all yell out,
"Cave in! Cave in!"
They start to shout!

Surrounding,
They throw their judgements on me;
I break as I contract the pressure on me.
I'm stoned in front of everyone,
and I don't want them to see!
"I'll be strong," I think.
"I will stand my ground," I speak!
*"I promised I'd stop,
even though victory is not free!"*

To be innocent,
I wish *I was*, at best,
Instead I hold such tenuous regrets on my chest.
*God, confront me,
Help me find my light,
Send me my message,
Let it be alright,
because the night is still searching,
and it can't find the day,
The gunshots keep flying,
While silently, I lay.*

Hide

The truth runs with my blood,
trots with horses in open fields,
caresses the slick skin of an animal deep in the sea.

No one really sees it,
my condolences continue to graze the top of the pond.

No one knows,
No one would bare to understand.
A battle of love and want.

The surface of my outer coat appears to be as is,
it camouflages me in a pack of traitors
dressed up as little kids.
I swim in the rivers of my being,
floating because I want to feel so light,
I am drenched as it starts to rain,
I begin to pour out my fight.

Playing hide and go seek with perfection,
amplified by the sun,
only the moon can see moments
for they are running water
seeping through open palms.

It is released in sweet redemption and tears,
through storms of merry shared by peers.

Troubles break like bread on the community table;
untouched,
She revels in the rain as salt,
So bitter to the taste,
yet garnishes the mind with relaxation…

for ghost stories, go to pg. 80

I See It

caught again...

As a spectrum holds of asked,
holds no screening,
such does a sunny cadence
tapped along with the soles of my feet.

Steady walking, steady swaying,
Steady hoping, recoil to praying.

For they view me as a mannequin
put out on display—
However, I happen to be alone
in my bedroom
writing to escape.

Being subjective to an ideology
that traps its own prey—
I have found electricity to be daunting
as it is all marked with a
touch of K.

To Live

Oh, to be the lightning bolt!
Shifting in the sight of drift,
Swimming to the outer lip—
Where words float to collective works.
Divine in recognition—
of simultaneous lines
Unfolding to be a spark
of Helix,
Untold in heavy pretense,
Face upon a sun
of where the fields go to carry young.

Life in words upon a screen.

Totemed Up Freestyle

"Again! From the top!"

Sitting on a plate,

like a notion or a nod,

sprouting forth & through,
as our cars drive us to their jobs.

It is odd, I think, pondering about a desk—
whilst reading about a raven, who made its fears into a nest.

I attempt to sketch conclusions,
That I keep boxed up & labeled 'vain'–
I forgot problems were the same as answers in this container made of rain.

Slowly gaining patience,
Putting negativity on mute,
Solely vines remember past endeavors,
Promising to reveal yourself to you.

Imagine all the dreams mined inside of you,
Picture that which you already know,
and depict that which you already knew.

Now, Rejoice in the complexity of a thought that is forever willing,
— to gamble — to stumble —
to forgive,
while still proceeding.

Because you cannot lose at a game you made with your own two hands,
And you cannot expect enthusiasm from a schedule filled with demands—

You may have heard it from me, or maybe through the grapes of time,
Paths, no matter which,
will lead back to the foundation of all rhyme—

I float like the lady,
Who collects society, tooth by tooth,
I ripple out inside the holy fountain, healing words used to age youth.
The water is clear, and the weather is fine,
come on in, the temperature is divine.

MADE IN SAME

Must we understand irony,
or shall it be just a game?

Some think I am ignorant,
some think, insane;

however, opinions are onions with an extra letter,

and I have forgotten how to be, *oh, so reserved.*

Tip goes the pen,

on top of a man-made disaster—

you may entice with aesthetic speech,

but my paragraphs grasp more matter.

I am honored to speak from a keyboard of sorts,

I am honored to be a female, living in an era,

where we may wear shorts!

SIMS

Swiftful and inappropriate,
Created and full of shit,
A rebound that fills up the space,
Actors that take the script at pace.

THE CLOSE OUT [STAY]
Looking at them
to only live your life
while inside your work.

TO BE BIRDS OF A FEATHER
A toast to Hamlet

The question prevailing life,
a question of who is free,
the existence or lack thereof,
is it worse to be or not to be?

Is a saint to subject himself to sitting silently,
while forfeiting his freedom to the fatal destiny?
Or shall he attempt to stand up,
and fight the force,
that writes the plans and designs the course?
And even then, the sea of discontent flows,
endlessly—
Does the trouble end with death?
Or does one wake again within a new reality?

To never sleep again,
One hopes forth to be,
A final destination for slumbering minds,
Not a dream within a dream.

Once done with the pains and chains attached to the physical body,
I dream of rest [a pause]
to freely breathe deeply.
Wanting, yet not sure when,
Match will come in the end,
but how will it greet? Will it greet at all?
The unknown makes the mind choose to
stagnate and stall.

Slowly losing actions course ——
If souls are in constant returning motion,
Let the memory of past sin,
be held behind
doors open.

THROUGH THE PINWHEEL

I'm a hungry buff,
Roaming the globe,
I've been searching for something
I've always owned—
But what's known is not
through the density of my skull.

I feel light of Heart in Mind,
but slowly down with time—
I go!

Some speak of moments,
I speak of passion,
In need of a certain peace,
Will only be brought in by action…
But who am I?
To be speaking out of loud—
Such proud and pre-cautious things.

I put meanings into words,
as if I know what they mean,
a word of a word,
thus brings
brink to a fact—
Do I lack
a single essence
or can I count on the words
flowing through
the false cracks?

A field is there,
I think,
No, I know.
Nothing is something,
Into the Void—
      I must go!

Deeper than before,
Four Score and Twelfth night ago—
Control
and
Control…
It speaks,
      I let go—

      My pen becomes Being.

Mighty is innate,
Flesh and blood,
Destroys ideologies
and sells them back to Future Fate
as mud.
If thou art made
of soot and dirt.
I wait,
as seed makes into bud.

Where am I?
and how can I pass,
Please,
May I through door?

Perception is mad!
It grabs
all things certain—
It veils me with indecision,
Accidentally,
I stab virtue
through this curtain.

What prevails at the end of this day?
A moment for rest
or a pause of dismay?

Despair
is so heavy
in the fields I travel—
Minutes are not time,
and time is not gravel.

Grand is one's intent,
As they trace all that is free.
Remember, Race
is not a race—
and to win
is not To Be.

Words from Brother
Anything that doesn't scale
has something functionally
wrong
with it

Words from Higher Self
Don't worry about forgetting
anything—— for all is just a
concept of
the plot

PORTAL - ABLE

Visualizing where I dream to be—

Whilst being there

is a mighty, mighty thing.

To stand on the teeth of description,

while maintaining my own integrity,

and learning to form a formation of foundation,

where my flow of knowledge

may develop into a stream.

I speak of illusions

that present themselves in farce.

I fear being replicated,

but then forget mine own

egotistical remarks—

To forsake my ship,

is not the same,

as blowing past echoes,

that whisper, *"Refrain."*

I am as powerful as the oceans

that receive the current of light

that bring inspiration into my lungs

and subconscious reflection,

I view above night.

"As Above, So Below!"

I bellow without fear,

Whilst creating a cradle—

I don't need,

to mask an invisible tear.

PERSPECTIVITY:
The Tale of The Queen & The Sad One

Choice is grace, love is elegance

"There is something in the air tonight,"

said The Sad One to The Queen,

"I was walking around outside and–"

She then proceeds to halt talking,

as The Queen lowers her head,

and whispers nonchalantly—

Something I cannot hear,

Since, I am just a distant observer writing.

A secret of the trade

—to share ideas without mocking—

.

Like a bird,

The Sad One begins to chirp.

She runs excitedly

to her palace balcony

on the Eastside of Brooklyn, New York.

———————————————————————

[Where I am, is where I am to be]

Words from Lover

I am sitting across from you,
Perpendicular to choice.
I am sitting next to you,
Unknowingly, we share
parallel voice.

Words from Sister

Sister,
Your voice
Speaks in rhymes.
Sister,
Your voice
is collective grace divine.
Sister of Mother,
I thank your ivory form,
For being of love,
For leading the course—
To tail the feather of living mind,
To trail the fluff of a head fed twice,
To keep the key-per open
is fine—
To look through mutual eyes,
Oh, be nice!

OXEN AND BUFFALO

May we treat with sacred medicine.
To out as mind that is to open—
To receiving and forgiving
the *as* of assumption.
    Fill up my cup with *retreatment*
    and knowledge to trust fate
    in forgo to function.
        To follow the clues of originating hate,
        To realize thou existence
        as a complete humanscape.
    To halt waiving and stalking,
    Leaving nothing to be in.
    On foot, in brightness, is illumination.
To hold the record and hold the lights,
To close thee eyes and relive the nights.
    Now, write it in stone and carve it in wrists,
    Wash from the blood and scratch on the list.
Surround yourself with Air,
and mind your canon,
    Let free your flaws,
    To impress the depression.
Watch the splash from
Above the Bridge
—instead of from the water,
    Remember in sweetness,
    The Earth is the Mother
of the Daughter.
Allow perception's door
to rejoin its hinge,
because life is not linear,
and pain is mirrorly [merely]
a reflection.

For if life is worth nothing,
should not one simply rejoice?
    Forth simple will become one
    with the oxen in your gin,
    and change towards the sun
        is better than where's been.

A STRIKE

I walked and I felt and
I was where you've been,
I stepped,
They followed,
The path to the bridge.
I stood on the Edge
and held all my breath
and was placed on the cusp
of where void went to rest.

I jumped to the wood and
looked among the gaps,
I held in my hand
and began to light the match.

I grasped a freedom
inside my head,
I lost my worries,
No finding Love's ledge.
The thought twisted,
breathed slowly down my neck,
It grabbed and forced me
into creating *an* Hex,
I've seen you,
I've heard you,
I've messed with
the dream,
I stood here and looked
at the stagnant little stream.
I've wondered if the ledge
has named you its price,
I've wondered if you could
would you show me light?
I've shook hands with risk,
I've wrestled sublime.
Now come here and listen:
No   "Figure"
I can't   "Through"
Love   "Time"

Silbury Hill

Things began to take hold
when she really took her life into her own hands.
She was young and spry
and quite ready to relieve her mind of such demands—
Her Kind was set on telling a story
about a boy
who she got to know
through the mystical endeavors
of allegory.

There are days that come and go like numbers.

8/8/13

Up til light—
Down til sun—
Underneath a bone,
Hid depth & one,
If to be there was to be,
Then I was existing—
Stuffed with clear communication—
and shared understandings of story.

Classic Fairytale

A Daisy & A Twig
I am nothing but a fool, caught in oblivion

I am the cusp of a cavity,
the eyelids of a whale,
a mind without the body,
I've become nothing but a tale.

I hold a compass in my palms,
with the thoughts of eventual novelette,
I am the person dedicated
to watching your green light
from the end of my deck.

I am in love with the near of you,
the lust of corroboration,
foe the monotony of fame,
go the ace of ascension.

I let myself behold the harmless bird,
you look mocking,
I am the leaves of the forest that
never outwardly die,
which the tabloids call *"shocking!"*

I am the Sunday of every weekend,
and the cloud of your faut,
I am the dreamer and the giver,
as I picture us melted together
in a pot.

I've become a lover of the stars
and a creator of space.
I am a catcher without the rye,
A flower looking for its
bookmark of lace.

I once forced my head
into a tiny cylindrical box,
A pattern with the aspiration
to find dedication
without getting caught.

Hold my hand as I turn the corner.

Look at me,
put your head on my shoulder…
*"Remain steadfast and listen, Honey,
soon you will be my only bunny."*

The Weatherman [HAARP]

The
Trees keep
following me
and won't leave me alone.
Overnight you try to reach me,
but I'm afraid I'm never home.
When I reply,
You always stray.
I want to be with you,
Every moment of everyday,
but the gap between hope and time
is beating me in stature.
At first, you confuse me
To the constant state of fracture;
I dream of a smooth, ever-present being,
But wake up to empty surfaces,
Searching for meaning.
I'm in love with a day I've never seen,
I'm in love with a sly, sly machine.

Mr. Right

INT. KATHLEEN'S HOUSE-DAY.

KATHLEEN opens the fridge and looks for her usual breakfast ingredients.

> KATHLEEN
> ...Hmm, what sounds good today? Ooh, milk...

She grabs the milk. All her movements are very refined. She then opens the cabinet on her left and reaches in for a box of generic cereal.

> KATHLEEN
> ...and cereal...

She seems rather unexcited but is still content. She sets the milk and cereal on the counter. KATHLEEN then walks over to the other cabinet and grabs a bowl.

> KATHLEEN
> ...a medium sized bowl of it sounds delicious.

She sets the bowl down next to the milk. She then walks back to the same cabinet to get a glass. She walks over to the sink and fills the glass with water. She sets the glass of water down next to the cereal.

> KATHLEEN
> Hydration... check.

She grabs a spoon from the drawer.

> KATHLEEN
> Utensil... check.

KATHLEEN walks back to the counter and sets the spoon down.

                    KATHLEEN
    This cereal is so bland... not even quite crunchy enough. Sometimes,
                I want to add sugar, but I don't.

KATHLEEN fills the bowl with cereal, closes the cereal, adds the milk.

                    KATHLEEN
                2 percent milk?... (sigh)
                 I thought I had 3 percent.

She closes the milk and puts it back in the same exact spot of the fridge as before.

                    KATHLEEN
         Maybe I was too harsh on the cereal earlier...
     I mean how bad can it really be? I eat it every morning,
     and I like most mornings, 16% of daily recreation... *what?*

She puts the cereal box back in the cabinet.

                    KATHLEEN
         ...it's not that bad. In-fact, it's great!

Then she picks up her made-bowl of cereal, glass of water, and spoon. She walks to the kitchen table sets the bowl, glass, and spoon down. Then she pulls out her chair and sits down.

                    KATHLEEN
                        Mmmm...

She begins to eat the cereal, but stops after her second mouthful.

                    KATHLEEN
                        Gosh...

She sets down her spoon, gets up and walks over to the drawer with napkins in it. She grabs a napkin.

                    KATHLEEN
                I don't want to make a mess.

She walks back, sits down, and starts eating again. She is in the midst of finishing her cereal when she hears a "cha-ching" noise. Confused, she looks around.

KATHLEEN
Was that the microwave?... Wait… no, I didn't prepare a Steam Food Pocket this morning...

She shrugs it off and assumes it was just her imagination. She gets back to her cereal. As she is about to take the next bite, she notices a new lamp to the side of the table.

KATHLEEN
...a lamp?...

She is confused. Then she is suddenly happy.

KATHLEEN
Great!

She sets down her spoon, and decides to switch the light on.

KATHLEEN
I knew all this room needed was a little more light.

She comes back to her cereal. She is pretty happy to have the new lamp, but she has no earthly idea where it came from. She finishes and puts her dishes in the sink. She looks out the window.

KATHLEEN
Such a beautiful day... The dandelions are really going to flourish this season!

She hears another "cha-ching", but this one comes from down the hallway, outside the kitchen.

KATHLEEN
Oh goodness, that noise again! I heard it...

She creeps towards the hallway. She is rather nervous of what she will find. She turns the corner, and there is a chair sitting in the middle of the hallway.

> KATHLEEN
> Velvet! Oh, that print.
> I adore the way it compliments the chair.

She sits in the chair.

> KATHLEEN
> I find velvet to always be rather plush.

Looks down at chair.

> KATHLEEN
> ...But a little too firm... and prickly...

She stands ups and looks at the chair.

> KATHLEEN
> It doesn't even match here.

She tries to move it, but it won't budge.

> KATHLEEN
> Ergggggg... Ughhhhh (Trying to move chair).
> Uhhhhhh... (Between breaths)
> Why… is ... this... so… heavy!

KATHLEEN gives up. She is annoyed. She storms off.

CUT TO:
INT. KATHLEEN'S BATHROOM-DAY.

KATHLEEN enters the bathroom and looks at herself in the mirror. She grabs her toothbrush and puts toothpaste on it. She turns on the sink and begins to brush her teeth, then she brushes her hair. She puts her hair up in a ponytail.

                    KATHLEEN
         Ah, I hope it's not too steamy outside the house today.

She walks to her closet, opens it, and grabs a pair of socks and shoes. She sits on the ground and puts her socks on, then she puts on each shoe and ties the laces in a perfect bow. She stands and then exits.

CUT TO:
INT. GARAGE-DAY.

KATHLEEN enters the garage. She grabs the gardening tools and seeds.

                    KATHLEEN
              Organic wheat barely, perfect.

She turns off the light and exits. As she is closing the door to the garage, she hears a "cha-ching" from down the hall. She is scared. She slams the door and runs down the hallway. She notices the chair has been moved and is now against the wall, along with another chair. Now, there is a sitting area.

                    KATHLEEN
         ...Oh, alright... Well, wonderful, that was exactly where I wanted to move it.

She sets the gardening tools down and sits in the new chair.

                    KATHLEEN
              Okay, this is rather comfortable.
              Nice shape, good cushion.

KATHLEEN then stands up, grabs the gardening supplies and walks towards the back-door. Right when she is about to grab the door handle, her arm snaps back down to her side, and she turns around. She sets the gardening tools down. She walks straight back through the hallway and up the stairs. She walks towards her bedroom.

CUT TO:
INT. BEDROOM-DAY.

KATHLEEN walks to the bed. She begins to make the bed.

                    KATHLEEN
...Ugh... I don't like making beds. Fold here, fold there, straighten the pillows, who cares, I'll be right back in it tonight.

KATHLEEN finishes and steps back to look at her bed.

                    KATHLEEN
                    (Admiringly)
...it does look nice though.

KATHLEEN turns around, walks out of her bedroom, walks down the stairs and the hallway to the backdoor. She picks up the gardening tools.

CUT TO:
EXT. BACKYARD-DAY.

KATHLEEN opens door walks out into her backyard. She kneels and starts gardening. All of the sudden she hears a loud noise. It sounds like a raccoon has gotten into her garbage. She looks up from planting. Her eyes are wide open.

                    KATHLEEN
            (Frightened, really scared)
Don't tell me it's another chair!

She begins to creep towards where the noise came from (to the right, behind the house). As soon as she turns the corner, she sees trash all over the ground. There is a envelope on top of the trash can. She slowly walks over. She opens the letter and begins to read.

KATHLEEN
Dear KATHLEEN McSIMONS, raccoons have gotten into your waste. Please remember to leave the cans out on trash days only to prevent further raccoons. Thank you.

The envelope and note then disappear into thin air. She is confused as she begins to walk back over to the part of the garden that she was previously working on.

KATHLEEN
I … I… I don't understand.

She kneels down to start gardening again.

KATHLEEN
I don't want to garden. I don't want to do this… I just don't understand! ... the letter? the envelope? I didn't even hear a raccoon... But then why was the letter there? And why I am still gardening?

She tries to throw the gardening tools down onto the ground. She cannot release the tools from her hand.

KATHLEEN
They won't budge!!! (Hysterical) I just don't understand!!!
If I don't want to plant, I should not have to plant. I want these tools out of my hands. I want my hands free. I want to go inside it is so hot...
IT IS SO WARM OUTSIDE. I WANT TO BE FREE.
(yelling now)
Let me free! Let me go!

At this point, KATHLEEN is waving her arms in the air and jumping up and down (tools still in hand). She tries to speak and yell out as loud as she can.

KATHLEEN
LET ME FREE! I WANT TO BE FREE!

CUT TO:
INT. MATT FOLENSBEE'S BEDROOM-DAY.

We see an over-the-shoulder shot of MATT playing The Sims computer game. On the screen, we see KATHLEEN jumping up and down, gardening tools still in hand. We overhear KATHLEEN screaming in some sort of Sims gibberish from the computer speakers.

                        MATT
          Time to make this bitch a boyfriend.

SCENE

Words from Friend

Start
writing
the book,
and let your future
unfold, consciously,
right before your eyes.

Words from Messenger

Take it
or
leave it,
but don't
just wait around.

Oh, Tweeze!

Fidgety is not something I am,
It is something I hold,
I act as if this timber's got a mould—
as if I am so unconveniently tame,
as if I get chopped down
and told to behave,
as if my page rages
from the left
of the right,
as if the morning wakes up to tip the night.

on the way to nyc

She Came in Through The Broken Arrow

The energy is my breath
that skates along wonders of the Earth.
It speaks the houses in character,
and brings graciousness as it returns,
To my lungs,
to fill me up,
and feed the plush of grasses,
To give abundance in redundance,
To feed,
and tend
the masses.

Love and Haight

I am You.

———————————

My cat's on the loose — found a moth round my head.
I promised to relax on the metaphors,
but that's how life goes after listening to The Dead.

Federal

I think I'm crazy,
but how would I know?
How I break down the symbols,
and return real slow;
My mind is a field,
and the words are the blooms,
I scatter in seeds that
relive high noon.

Stoned Gold Fox:

Echoes in movement of the self,
Brings about the idea of beings felt.
Doting as scintilla of an empire,
"Broken to build,"
Reports the squire.

5-Point Star

It is admirable,
It is just,
It is within—
The idea of trust,
To be in vine,
To be of such,
To be the sun giving the moon a hug.

11:11

I wish to be tall when I walk,
and I wish to be
as such trees,
appointed with the anointment of wisdom,
and bringing truth in projecting—
I wish to be
full of love in my heart;
I wish to be
the beauty of art;
I wish of health,
and I wish of pleasure,
I wish to make each moment the gold I treasure.

sings of (⌘) writes of

Possible Band Names

Illegal allies, Legal immigrants

You divided by Me, Myself

Daze & Knights [Days & Nights]

From Your Dreams...

Sounds of Golden Amber

Up on The

Clouds that Could

Woodstock and Melting Stones

The Age of Fluff

Fluff 'n Gold

Back to Base

The Only

Free-will, Walls

Of This & That
Within, Withdrawn

Muse in Liquid

Honest

Bread + Butter

*Full of
Our Own*

Couch

*From The End
Creative Beginning*

*The House of Argumentatives
The Home of Representatives*

Sunny Day

Of Vine

*Additional Vices
Advice in Costume*

Tamed to the Common Eye

Created, Loved

Solidity, Fluidity

Signature, Metrical

Ripe: Live from The Garden

The Politics of...

belay's on,
play on

Bridge 6

There's 16 bars, round the block,
Call it verse, I hit the parking lot
—And heads start to reverse.

The 4 x 4s
Shaking down every measure,
Where the beat shadows the rhythm,
Setting tone for the weather.
Whether this,
or whether that,
It's either or
it's all—

Who is integrity,
To set up the pieces,
but not to answer the call?

- — - — - — -

The Ides of Joy

My intention is for the peaceful gathering
of my words
& other sounds,
through means of voice.

- — - — - — -

Songstress

There's voice in my Breath,
every thought,
I move,
I Breathe.

- — - — - — -

Sing a slow one,
It's not about the chords this time.

Welcome, This is A Wheelhouse

There is a foundation that ebbs and flies,
With the intention of signaling motive within tribe,
Fro the bird that mocks the wind,
Flow of bout as thunder water bends,
Air the wheel rolling down the mountain,
Spurs the spoke telling yonder fountain,
To rock the boat as fellow to sun,
To place the music in garden of young.

Go forth in concert
Is the spirit of fun,
Run four!
Twice more!
Together as one !!

Listen!
Listen!
Hear!
Hear!
Reveal to soul
The line to appear.
Prance on, Droplet,
And bellow a plenty!
Open your eyes,
The world is friendly!

MSG
6:58 pm
12/30/16

THE GHOST

Started waking up early,
so I could get some rhymes down,
skipping phrase to phrase,
no seconds left for time out.

Sitting in the stands — started ruffling my feathers,
got so many opinions,
but to my soul
they ain't tethered.

I speak as I flow,
so I glow as I breathe,
I decided for one life,
started talking with the trees.

Falling like leaves,
they come to my paper,
calling to my eyes,
myself as self to savor.

I've been around, round the block before,
where the moments meet the grass,
burning sage to clear of field,
as I sit and listen to the voices of the past.

Within is without,
a promise I can make you;
see and believe,
I tap the beat with my shoe.

I am naming the mix master,
the origin of feats,
put your hands together,
voice your thoughts from the streets.

It's to be a grand one,
It's to be better,
It's to reach inside my mind,
and choose grace over matter.

It's to put my own hand
over the air I breathe,
and consequently, choose,
to stand up,
instead of leave.

Raining from the sky,
like water ought to be,

opening new paths—

It's priceless to be free,
It's mindless to exceed,
the bandwidth of your need,

a spoken nod of conscious agreement,
forsaken love often turns to greed.

SEVEN SISTERS, ONE PACT.

I'm bringing words
Standing for my underconscious;
Those moments where I danced forth
To reel in knowledge.
No longer gripping to the grain
of another lost man,
Who claimed green[ery]
is for paper
rather
than inhalation.
My lungs grow deep
With the roots
That sing upon the Åir—
That draw my motions
out from the
shadow
of despair.
I seek to speak from
the eyes of
a different day,
That which is of this moment
in every Witch way.
To float,
I fall
in hovered scores:
4 years today,
7 sisters strong.
We know we're onto
the network
with the latest news—
Channel 11,
broadcasting a
second parallel to you.
To awareness, I support,
when my retinas scanned the room
listening for relative context—
I find,
[1/29/16]   my perception is tricky.
[4/4/17]   *It was a long strange ride.*

Ode to Dancer

Degas you a question, homie?

> Pauses & stops,
> plus maintaining grip,
> moments arriving,
> *bliss in movement!*
>
> When along with the music,
> a dancer, She glows,
> with a sense of eased time,
> and a depth of unknown.
>
> Calm and blithe,
> plus fulfilling all flown!
>
> *We remember!*
>
> And, so we thank
> those who move
> to the rhythm
> of their own soul.

Spirituous —

Not just about time and space,
but about the use of written spatial moments,
outlined in the transitive format of time.

Golden Chaos

There's a girl,
who walks in a field,
surrounded by flowers
She can only feel.

Free from the sunset
that falls on her back,
She dances
and sings
every word on the track.

The moon is her light
of a loving composer,
Filling the beat
with sounds
of the slumber
drifting closer.

Finding the shore
And the tide that chose her,
She lives in the sunshine,
And the beauty it
shows her.

Plato's Chair

I search,
glance around my surrounds—
As if — what I seek
lies outside my bounds.

Ode to Healer

Promise :
*I will stand for cultural growth
through understanding my own
perspective on solidity.*

*I will heal the wounds of my
current life, and I will
synchronize this healing
with those around me,
causing a ripple effect.*

*I will use words to speak
knowledge, and I will
not use words to manipulate;
I will sing of Joy!*

Chant :
*My vision is not imaginary;
it is my imagination
that provides the fertile soil
for my vision to come into fruition.*

THE SOCIOLOGY OF STARING

times & minutes & colors,
something amidst the foundation of others,
startles to learn, startles to touch,
what is a basis without some semblance
of a crutch?

sparked within a tiny, tiny being,
seeing & feeling & reaching
— completing —
strangers to learn, *stop*, strangers to touch,
what completes the basis of knowing
what is gained and what is lost?

GET OUT OF MY LABORATORY

If contentment is just a moment
within this colossal waste of time,
then courageous actions are diabolical;
to stab my back,
you must take your place in line.

Glimpses and glances,
People and trees,
I contemplate the outline of your torso
and all the taxes and hidden fees.

To hold your heart with sorrow
and see it with remorse,
I catch my mind looking back
at something that came out of force.

If love is now
and love is thee,
I am here for you now
to evaluate me.

I

Inhalation,
Dimensions,
The turn around…
Traces,
Freckles,
Surrounding voices of a shroud.
Concentricities among young
and Whispers amongst listeners—
Come towards the light,
as we confess to said sinners:

Circle rale gonish
And gibbish gamoodish!

Reflecting her among apples
and peaches with Prudence.

Staying stands in the wind,
Along with the broodish,
Following their faces
And copying said mooses;
Whom of habit and
of rabbit,
Whom of love and
of above,
Turns to Air,
And simply,
Shrugs ?

Words from Chief
The year is 1999, and we are just now coming to see, the chair still has 4 legs.

Words from Stranger
You are a connector.

IMPOSSIBLY [LOUVRE]

Corrupt to the bones,
Entranced with a facet,
Harnessed to notions,
Production becomes habit.

Formation to format,
Life to word,
Followed by Fife,
I am followed by a herd.

Selection amongst identities—
I've imagined a changing,
Surrounded by lovely — *Surrounded by facing.*

Past, truth, now and here,
Listen to the words,
As they entice your ear.

I had become distant, remorseful,
lacking,
— *in-fact;*
outline my words
and step up to bat.

Induction,
Being,
Seeing,
Believing:

I'm a word to a page,
A thought to a noise,
A regret to an apology,
The plot to certain ploys.

I hate Truth!
I loathe it!
I swallow it whole!
I breathe it,
As I taste it,
Then rejoice in its song!

I am joyful
That you and I remember
Breath for who she is—
A chance to understand
The Love that gives.

- — - — -

Make a prediction right now:
Time will repeat,
and the generations will rise
and live in it knowingly.

- — - — -

"Let's order a pizza."
"Nah, let's save $ for acid!"

- — - — -

WITH THEE

It could be
Just like this.
Your breath
On my wrists.

As if,
My voice weighs
Heavy
On his mind.

As though,
Seconds
Made sense of
Time.

SUNDAY, MUNDANE

You make me feel like bread,
when you cut me up,
You tear me into slices,
and feed me to ducks.

FROSTY

Let's have some fun,
before I melt away.

EGGS AND BACON

You got me feeling so toasty,
and that is just what I need,
To be held in your phalanges
and given ways to breathe.

THE GOLDEN DICTIONARY (TICKET)

I have not seen any limitations thus far.

PUSHING FLOWERS

I love you,
I cannot.
I love you,
face in knots,
mind in wonders,
land in time,
pass my eyes,
and tickle me with lies.
I love you,
I love you not!
I say this twice,
even after we have fought.
Not to be - I laugh in sight,
transposing character
as dignity gains light.
I love you,
stop, I cannot.
For if it is simply so,
I'd love you
as much as
I love pot!

She continued to leave herself open,
only saying goodbye with words.

SOMETHING OVER NOTHING
The Teenage Years

Under siege, marked a girl, surrounded by mirrors. She sat inside the dimly lit room and stared at the mirrors. As the candle steadily melted, she sat in the corner, staring at the mirrors. Through the sound of the night and the passing of the train, she remained on the floor, staring at each mirror. She could hear the sound of her childhood, beckoning from outside the wall; grasshoppers and catfights, she missed the loud hisses that lulled her to sleep. She let her eyes frolic amongst the reflecting walls. She let her mind slip into a new world. She let her thoughts dangle and loiter inside this world. Dripping like wax, the concepts ran through her brain; the girl pondered about the decisions that she would someday have to face. She let her head float, as it tried to comprehend the existence of her place on earth. She took out some paper and watched her fingers move swiftly among the lines of the page as she wrote down, "This world…" She felt strange being alone with no one to look at but herself. Drawn to her reflection, she swore to keep starving her ego. Watching her hand move in time with the words, her nails glimmered in the flickering light as she wrote down, " is about floating between what's real and what's absurd." She looked up from her paper into the mirror. She needed to look herself dead in the eyes, so that her thoughts could catch up with the passing time. Staring deep into her pupils, her focus darted between the left and right. "Why do I have two eyes?" she started writing beneath line one of the paper. "What's the point of two eyes, when they are always looking at the same thing? What's the reason for my lashes, when they are something I cannot see?" She pauses for a moment and looks back to her reflection. She sees another girl standing there, but looks down and only sees legs and arms and toes and feet. Still rising into this question filled realm, she frantically scribbles down, "I cannot see the real me, just this reflection staring at me here." It's on the tip of her tongue, as she tries to translate the dilemmas that occupy her head. The echo between each canal of the empty cavity of her state of mind seemed to scream, telling her to *stop thinking*. She crouches in distress and wonders about the beyond. She lets her sight wander down the flesh of her arm. Nourishing her soul, she lets her sight walk down to her fingers, for they are clenched in a fist. She allows her confusion to come out and play. She grabs her pencil and writes hastily, "Why were we made this way? Why do I have ten fingers, and why do I have ten toes? What is the reason behind bone structure, and why are these the words that I have chosen? Why does my face have to stay plastered to my head? What is the difference between life on Earth and life being dead? Are the cells filling my cavities just lies I need to hear? Do they somehow help me understand my existence? What is behind my face? Is it a brain with an existing conscious? Why do I speak and how is it possible to form words with my mouth? How do I put together letters so that sentences come out?" She begins to chase after those moments when she actually knew what it meant to be alive.

As she looks around the room and glances in each mirror, she waves a pleasant *'hello…'* For maybe, there is truly someone in there! Overwhelmed with the concept of living just as a small being, she blinks her eyes and opens them wide. She writes down her realization. "Everything and everyone is just a thing." As her hand molds the words clear across the page, the girl questions sanity and realizes her mind is locked in a cage: A bird stuck in its own cocoon or a butterfly left to die alone in its nest. She was forsaken, and it felt as though she had always been. She writes again, "No matter what I learn there is always more out there. No matter what I understand, there is always something I cannot. No matter how many questions I ask, I will always be left in some sort of confusion. For right now, I have reached the world of *'nothing'*. My body has reached the place where I can feel my chest growing lighter. I have reached the place where I wonder why I am here and why I have each desire. I am now in the realm of questioning all I know. I have been locked in the place where forgotten seconds go." She scribbles faster, discovering incomprehensible things. Her arms slip away, as she becomes distracted by the itch on her lip. All she can think about is scratch, scratch, scratch. Scratching out her thoughts, she runs her fingertips across the bumps along her knee. "Why do I feel sensations, and why do emotions reign my actions? Why do I feel towards anything? What is the point of all these interactions? One day, I won't stand anymore, and one day, I won't breathe. One day, the future will be more than just a date, and one day, I will realize that all I care for is to leave. Someday, I hope to fill the gaps in my mind, because in this reality, everyone is blind." The girl closes her eyelids and raises her hands to cup her brain. She feels the indentations of her temples, as her thoughts try to wrap around time. Once again, she stares at the creature of a reflection. She wrestles with the beast's movement as each girl lifts her right arm and left arm in sync. "Why is my head placed on such a body? Why is the universe so large, and I'm just some tiny nobody? Why was I granted the ability to think? What is the motive behind every word I speak? Are these my ideas, or is every person just a story that has already been told?" Slowly, she stands from the blank corner of her mind, she steps forward to the candle; trying to discern reality, she sticks her finger in the flame. Is it her mind that is panicking or is she really in pain? The heat from the newly formed burn radiates through her ring finger. She decides for today that she is still alive, so she walks back to her paper. She flips over her pencil and erases all the questions that her naïve-self previously said. She looks in the mirror and decides, "Well, at least I am not dead." She opens her mouth and searches for sense in anything. She asks the girl, staring straight into her eyes' windows, "What is the purpose of you?"

And on the piece of paper she carves, *"Nothing."*

ACT PRETTY

Light headed and eager,

to see something I cannot see.

The epitome of a loner,
"THE WORLD REVOLVES AROUND ME !"

But the ego greets—
and tackles the only light left in my soul.

I must remember to be conscious—
of the actions I convey through my tone.

I say, *"I am sorry,"* again and again,
but only my head is free…

Therefore, I must contemplate—

Why to speak, if all I talk about is
the way I think things shall be.

It is me and me and me
in relation to you.

It is anguish beneath my eyes
as your heavy feet enter the room.

For, I am the creation of others,
and I hate what they have done.

I am an exaggerated being filled up with
angst in each lung.

ROTATIONAL RETURNS
[REACH THE SUMMIT]

Fear doesn't exist
without the mind.
Relative to where you stand—
It becomes a mirage;
A place you float to when your blood's not at ease.
You'll stand in your stance
and question motives.
You'll stand around the place
that provoked such pressure,
such tension in your arms.
Numb with extortion,
Your toes turn to bricks.
Fickle with fascinations,
Your mind scrolls
through possibilities.
Every brustle of the air,
Jolts intentions through your bones.
You creak with fright,
as you slander excuses.
You creak with slight enjoyment as
surprise awakens your senses!
You fondle the chances
to hold escape
over surprise.
It cripples your eyes
right back down to your heels…
becomes friends with
your marrow,
snap Remember, what it is to feel!

THE SEAL

Realization
Steps into the light.
She steps out of her body,
once more to fight.
She stands still at a road of choice,
Not fear.
She stands still because numb has
stabbed her ability to hear.
She can't hold the amount in her shaking dusty hand.
She can't keep firing
because the winter stole Her plan.
She can't step forward to a place
with The End.
She can't step back,
because confusion has become
her friend.
She can't close her mouth,
because it's expelling calculated lies.
She can't close her head,
because she's feeding it alibis.
Realization to Recognition,
She forms the clouds
swarming over her mind.
She can't just realize,
it's getting colder with time.
She can't get back in the body she has left,
so She unlocks the Key to her Quest.
She keeps hitting her arm
and looking into her eyes.
She keeps trading her distance
for the Right to break Ties.
She keeps clothing choice
with a pair of nose
it never knew.
She keeps shaking decision
with hope of depleted solemn few.

She places her toes
inline with the vacant body ahead.
She places her vision
on the Dream assumed dead.
She slowly taps on the windows and
fishes for response.
She remembers the words,
She remembers just once.
She remembers the people surrounding her nest.
She remembers the eggshells she treaded on
to reach the Desk.
She remembers the Joy of a-founding the Mile.
She remembers the dilated crowd of pupils.
She remembers the Breath
before losing the marbles.
She plays with the idea of opening the past.
She toys with a personality that's bound to last.
She brushes the strand of hair from her face.
She remembers the look,
She remembers the place.
She stops her tape at the Present,
in The Now.
She slaps her face
with the Wind somehow!
She reaches in her mouth
and counts out her prize.
She pushes herself for
her remarks up High.
She touches a surface
that is sharper than
reality is.
She breathes in a mistake.
She reminds,
She's only a kid.

[8/09]
[August 2009]

MOUNTAINOUS GIRL [LOVE IS VALLEYS]

I become a cliffside,
To divine and douse upon.
I, a second in your spine,
A flash in your eyes.
I'm a burning of your past.
I'm a girl,
I am here.
I am here to last.
As I creep to the bridge
of your nose,
I become a member,
a loner to be exposed.
I am here,
I am here as Now.

So caress this moment
for it is all you will hear.
Caress the moment, the second,
Love in dear.

OVERHEARD

Someone told me once that
loneliness was failed solitude.
If loneliness was failed solitude,
then *what was I?*
What was I?
What was I to you?
A semblance, a past?
I'm asking you to tell me.

Reminder,
remind her.

DEGRADE A BEEF

Awake, staying

Don't think it is justifiable to end up all alone. I did this to myself; forgive me, I know. I think within my world, and I live within my oven. I fill it with biscuits growing towards the gates of nothing. It's sorrowful when you realize all you can do is express with words. I want to choose something else, yet I think of only awkward. I reverse to the beginning where life was before; I disappeared into thin air; I was prone across the floor. I become primitive, and boys become smart; they taught me that in school, right from the start.

LYING TO YOURSELF:
FOR DUMMIES

1st. Picture your past and consider your future.
Remember to realize exactly where you are standing for this, too, is important.

2nd. Take a millimeter of a step back.
Really look at yourself in that silly mirror.
It could be a portal to another world, but for now,
I will just go along with the theory that it is me… my reflection.

3rd. Account your friends and account your passions.
Do the components greet a completion of whole?

4th. See yourself for the boundless individual that you are.
Easily shifting, easily shaping, quick to hear the river's creek.

Where do my feet go?

THE SONG

Loafe with me on the grass,

Loosen the *stop* from your throat.

This too shall pass,

For all is remote;

Yet, The Dead lay ahead,

One deep, all alone.

"Remember to stay fed,"
Said the little girl,
Who was corrupt to the bone.

The Girl with the Tambourine

Theoretical explanations of thus that brings me down—

    is up,
    when I circumnavigate the town.

Upon arrival at the gates to Pearl's door,
    I reconcile the ideal of favorites
        And favors of ideas I ignore—

        Chance is exactly of opportune,
        Quite giving of love,
            Quite loving of broom.

        Shedding contrite understandings
           of a plot,
        Shared over the fire
        of nights in the lot.

            Joy runs by...
          And heirs her loom...
      She picks up the ceremonial drum...
Over tea this high noon.

Interdimensional Fable

Centurions of intelligence available to me,

Founded on recognition and full of remedy,

Loving and peaceful and light full at that,

Addled and reasoned and ready to be exact.

The sound of the ocean is the mountain playing to me,

is the sound of the breeze that passes in melody,

And the best of the best is the bear dancing,

Prancing toward the shadow

Brightening the fellow tree.

the longest rant, you've ever read
the longest rant, you'll ever read

A Thinking Place

I had been avoiding the words to say
as a mannequin to the crowd.
I was hiding from the barriers,
who hid from the hound of self.
Who was I —
To speak up to
A silly idea
of a caterpillar renting out a mushroom?
And in the woes
of the *oh's*
of time,
Who was I?
Oh,
Who was I?

      Pause to break—
      Pause to rest—
      Pause to take a gander
      from the tease of breast…

And —
Who are you?
I ask out loud.

"A sift through lyrics,
and a reverie in the propositional ground."
Who was I?
Who felt too much,
Who took the meat to make the brunch,
Who stood in the truest of the blue,
Who spoke in my rhymes,
And took up too much room.

Invisibility
spoke to me
in the silence
of drama destined,
and told me to stay on broadcast
and to the future always question.

I was trying to avoid
whilst abiding the stance of bones.
I was trying to portray
the reverence I condone.

Who am I?

A lamb on the precipice of furtive honesty.

Who to be?

A skeleton rocking the beads of rosary.

Melt

The breath of your eyes runs along the slope of my nose,

and the hopes of my thoughts drown under the stance you composed.

On the tip of a tongue, you created ice of my mind.

You dangled trust amongst unstable and whispered wants of mine.

Created of redemption,

and filled up with despair.

I watch as correction passes up all deemed perfectly fair.

Hearts turn to rubble,

as past turns to forget.

I start to stumble,

as Winter begins to tempt.

I watch as my feet step and step into tangle.

I watch as you leave my head out to dangle.

The present, the past, the face of attempt,

The want, the angst, searching for content.

Dripping from the lashes of a consumable thing,

Doting amongst the traces, as if I am a being.

Reaching for an answer to embark my precious whim,

Rounding the pasture for a stare that engulfs him.

Lingering turns to fulfilling,

and trotting turns to sane.

I pour moments out of my memory,

as I crumble in the rain.

Zero marks my feet, as I reach for your hand.

Twice towards the grip, as a shepherd judges his lamb.

I melt onto the ground,

A place meant for dead.

I trip onto the memory, a place your pupils left my head.

I followed you to the brink of a man made disaster.

I followed with close gaze, as you lope away faster.

Ignorant to the neurons surrounding my strain,

Unaware to the feelings, as chess is played with pieces of my brain.

and the circles around your windows keep darting out of mine,

and the clouds spoke of destiny to a little girl, who was fine.

I was trying to climb out of the emptiness of desire.

I was trying to surface from the corruption of a liar.

Plotting my letters with the knowledge of time,

Placing my nails in between each notch of said spine,

Spilling shared secrets and telling of a crime,

Ripping off my face, as I left myself behind.

Everyday is a day focused on tomorrow.

Volunteering towards a cause who fits the prospect of sorrow,

and I don't want to speak to the mirrors anymore,

and I don't want to be fed lessons I've already heard,

and I still just want to sense the thoughts presented so fast,

and I still want to look at you and feel the hope of all to last.

I still want to run around the imagination of above;

I still hold the snake that drips the venomous blood.

Standing on the box containing words put to bed,

Pulling all the puppets attached to the strings in my head,

Strolling through the seconds, where a simple glimpse stopped time,

Walking through the minutes where it was only you and I.

Guided towards a season,

My experience could not fit,

Tentative towards the night,

Time in a state of omit.

Developed in a span, sliced with light,

Moulding the future with choice in my sight.

Hearing a voice from the inside of my ear,

Sifting my fingers through the attempts of a whole year.

I still care for the canoe that forms from your toes.

You still control my pulse with the absorption of my foes.

I've memorized your palm as it told me goodbye.

I travel in dreams with the swiftness of a spy.

A SERIES OF SELF: KENDRA, PT. I

Part one of Me, Myself, did not much mind.

I started a new routine,

where I live each day one toe at a time.

I pick up one foot and then set it down. I pick up the other,
and next thing you know,

this Me is the talk of the town.

One toe here and one toe there…
Then She sees, surrounding her toes
are eggshells, everywhere.

PROCESSING THE NEGATIVES

I talk like a fool.

WHILST IN THE FICTION OF SKELETAL MEASURES: SONNET I

When lost within my gazing time,

Still I stare, though you, you burnt light,

bound to be delicate, decadent is thine

To be of dust and guitars, did thee even fight?

Sense from scents familiar, I manifest

of land, of root, of dripping, now of hand-me-down.

The grip of said pencil, you wrote next.

Just wading in eyes of brown,

My mouth, spilling hypocrisies,

step past petty time, seconds are triggering,

ever, for never, stealing my lies.

I said, she will not *stop*, if she is in the ring.

For together, we lock in presence, daze,

Can see an exit, but I am stuck in a maze.

[January 31, 2014]

¿DÓNDE ESTÁ MÍ CABEZA?

It was a concept,
Just a thought,
To become organized,
not stuck between motive and plot—
—So, I welcome you,
to my hood,
—— >> My Writer's Block

DEAD FISH

laundry - tube - cutoff shorts
- hoods -
low-key chores

commercials & fat
radiant!

but mixed up - plurality

abnormal - regular memories
are great, of course

but I found myself in
uncovered dirt—

— thus, disconnecting the hoodie
from the sweatshirt

WILL, SON!

Radiant is thou, wafting through the forest;
I remember the time
we pranced around fellow tourists.
I judge when I live,
so I think while I breathe.
I dislike a taste for negativity,
& question my pity for the green—
Where are the echoes?
Must I always pick up on the universal radio?
Over & out, the channel of thought,
I guess I'll release
that which I cannot.
'Tis no big deal,
a rod of lightning stole my face,
woke with the sun on my back,
no more doubt to trace.
I am certain in hope & reality,
I enjoy, very much, the skinny elephants of Dalí.
If big were the picture, where would I be?
Lost in a maze —
or lounging in Chekhov's cherry tree?

THE DREAMER'S LAMENT
could we trust that which we should be

It looked strange when I first found out my hands were made of dust,
feathers & dust,
dusty moments
are hard to trust;
this is true,
but where do we find ourselves?

The moon sets itself upon the sky,
without denial or chance to defy;
branches are busy growing,
& I want to be as such,
growing towards the sun,
because I tell myself so—

I can feel my
cells collapsing
into a new state
of traffic—
collisions turn into
electricity & I can feel it in my veins.

Hollow bones tell me to pulse,
& I know, so *I move;*
I cannot stand still,
I am not stagnant without you,
nor am I flowing in ways always just.
I've been waiting for your voices,
& your eyes tell me I must—
so I tackle my mind & save it up,
because a labyrinth is a labyrinth
from dawn till dusk.

MARK OF THE TRADE

*Sung, while lifting feline in the air.

It's the flower of life,
It's the wheel of fortune.

x 3

LADY JUSTICE
Wake up in the late afternoon

If truth is this & I am that—
what is matter, when dependent on fact?

If belief is knowing that you know that you know—
then why waddle in doubt yet feel comfort alone?

Many poems on my minds & words from my soul,
that get covered in cheese & fall right off the bone.

I found myself in Summer—
a place I hold so dear!

A time to toss frisbees one-handed,
with the other
holding a beer.

A SERIES OF SELF: KENDRA, PT. II
As seen in your dreams

I'm just a girl
and my intentions were good
I begged
and I pleaded
but I was not to be stood
under I went to my own little tunnel
where I climbed and I climbed
til I was caught and put back in my kennel
to be taught a lesson
that I already knew

was shameful and blameless
because I do what I do

888 - 555
Welcome to the family

Paranoia doesn't even begin to cover it,
but Pronoia is closer than a universe willing to fight against fate.

To be peaceful in transaction of energy is much more whole & round
than creating a truthful conspiracy.

To be filled with woes wouldst not be me,

To be radiant with colors would be much more grounding.

So I imbibe in myself,

& so do you,

Because I am my biggest fan,

& so are you.

SUGAREE

Many say my mind's a pilot,
"To where do we go on this
spaceship united ?"

"To get ice-cream with cookie dough
all layered up with choco choco chips."

"To make sure you get your fill
of the chaos that gets your trip !!"

Fueling,
Straight drooling,
For the next one.

The next song that assures me
I have floor tickets instead of lawn.

Traveling,
Remain standing,
For you're the one to play.

The next song that sings,
"I'm on two or three speakers
placed on different markers of delay."

SUMMER

The furthest away

are the people I love.

The people I love,

are the furthest away.

— K

BUTTERFLYS* WITH BANDAGES

Alisa Fedele performing with Heaps n Heaps

Time is a garden,
bigger than we know…
To pick all the weeds,
I'm gonna need all my Hoes!

A SERIES OF SELF: KENDRA, PT. III

I decided it was time for a change.

I didn't just want cents anymore.

A SERIES OF SELF: KENDRA, PT. IV

I just didn't know the backbone of solitude was being alone.

PANORAMA'S BOX

We'll call it a tank party!

In such quarters,
we plant & water with the words of Me.
Sing,
to sing of our inevitable horizons,
thus sprouting forth into a land of liberty!

I may turn, to turn, to move,
& end up in 360°,
The collective act of actions,
reveals truth in actuality.

Falling into focus,
we wake up by name,
which makes waiting at the Great Golgi Gate,
never again quite the same!

To be packaged & heard,
like a true metaphor,
to pick up your stuff & march right out that door!

To hear it is of one,
but then to listen to the other,
To rose & to muse the sweet orange
of thunder.

Another day,
Another voice heard,
It was you,
but it was me,
& you were swimming like a bird.

It was as if you could leave,
but always come back,
or remain in two places,
I am still confused by that.

INVOCATION OF SOUL, BY SELF

Dancing within the broken spires that speak of stones once frozen,
I awaken my knowing of compassion,
and my ability to feel passion for the chosen.

I am free from the self I constructed,
out of the plastic of used spouts.
I feel the elasticity of my muscles,
as my choice ignites the composition
of a destiny disguised as a dream
I hung up to dry on my shelf.

To dust off my boundaries,
I see the limitations for the presumption they once did project.
I witness the comfort of thus, surrounding my circumstances in jewels
of illusory themes of debt.

To owe not a nickel,
but only the sense of my dual depth;
I disentangle my notion of a signature within a multidimensional contract,
penned by the hand of thine own words in text,
and signed atop the surface of my own cedar wood adorned desk.

Rise to rise,
I burn the cents we need to connect,
by co-creating artificial realities that expose the exploration of the goddess of death.

We gather in colors,
to shade in the lines our ancestors protect.
We are woven together,
to create the shared tapestry of social and locational context.

JEDI MIND BRICKS
[JET EYE MINED FIX]

I was feeling past Barstow,
due East,
I was searching for the weather
on a map of the Bee's Knees—

The hippest sketch in town,
To navigate me >>
Back to the senses
I assumed
had abandoned me - - - -

But what an ass of mine is you,
when I choose to assume,
that I ever let my feet
walk me out of the room.

I grow and wander in *consciality,*
I pick up my choices
at 8,
to celebrate our anniversary.

.

SMARTER THAN THE AVERAGE ELEPHANT

Babar comes to mind, as I try to avoid another conversation with an unavoidable

human being. Is it just me and myself, trying to figure out resent versus escape?

Am I entrapped within a body that is not mine; am I simply a soul that will remain the wandering kind? I *stop* and look at the notes I've written mindlessly and stuffed into my brain. Consumption of confusion, I am a featherless bird locked in a cage— I am naked towards the public and blow up your inbox with rage.

Stop, look, don't listen… I swear, I am too insane.

At age 5, I learned that I would grow up to be a freak on display. 5 dollars for a quick peek, but it is free if you'd care to stay. I have enough space in my cell for multiple personalities. We can stack person atop person and call it a game.

At 16, I realized I was alive to die. Reckless amongst my aspirations, I lead most to run far and fast from me. They leave afraid.

I'm not saying that Shirley was not a shrimp or that I can locate a dagger within

a dungeon, but my voice is here for a reason, and I'm sorry, buddy, but I ain't leaving.

————CONTORT————

Ba, ba black sheep,
I'm coming for your wool.
I'm searching for your thoughts,
and digging around your skull.
LET me in,
Let me touch the stem behind your eyes;
Let me see your inner workings,
Stop hiding in disguise.

You're so lucky,
You have a mind that fits your body.
Mine is filled with air
and cream cheese.
It giggles when I think,
and bubbles with discovery!
I would give you a peek,
But then, I must also provide recovery.

THE BUTTERFLY EFFECT
Written May 24, 2009

Life is something that can never —truly— be caged and bottled.

Something holding no familiar territory, yet it can be sold in seconds with just a glance.

—— >>>

… Thoughts trickling towards a stream of pastimes [past times] and anxieties…

… Pours out into an open surface of actions paired with despair…

The scene is set amongst characters who seem to each play a vital role,

but actions turn to moments,

and moments turn to memories—

Folding and tracing regrets in your palm,

feeling and caressing the storm before the calm.

Creating new molecules,

by means of each breath of each day,

becoming New Poems,

upon every self-crystallizing mistake.

Leading the follow

with a face set in stone,

blossoming as a shroud

with the forever unknown.

Hearing each sound above the current's dancefloor,

re-living every juncture

through open eyes

described as doors.

Oh, Sweet and Joyous Butterfly!

Please, prepare me
for the gift of
my own wing-set.

Today and everyday,
teach me
to let living
be my effect.

GOOD IN THE HOOD

Thought to be sour,
Thought to be sweet.
Thought to be going without any of my means—

Outside myself,
Living onshore,
I left myself behind—
Until I found myself chillin' next door.

TO BECOME THE WORD PROCESSOR
FT. KENBUNNY

No one was handing me a microphone—
So, I decided to make my own—
First, I considered a Soapbox
much more pretentious
and friendly,
but you're right—
If I really want fans,
I have to celebrate spontaneity.

For (4),
Me is I,
and I is You.
I am here;
this is one another,
yet truth.

BERTHA

Jumping of my bones
From the sands I left behind,
From the seconds
Cloaked in dusty spells
I swear I could define.

Rite by write,
I took the letters
that fell into my head…
… and formed them into future
… treads (don't).

STEVIE WINDWOOD
[HAND ME THE GUITAR]

I sing,
I chant,
I play,
I return.
The chord of invention,
I inscribe in my journ;
I dance as life would
That turns about face,
That glorifies each ear in its sonic intake.

THE LOT

I brought paint.

9 in a Bottle

I wanted to come about myself,
before the big burn,
where we all take turns
being the mocking of the bird.

I've thought about love,
but I've never felt any such mental state—
I was stagnant,
like a snake,
with no legs to breathe
or reach for my pedestal,
where I actually understand my dream.

Nor concentrate,
for such is that,
and experience is so—
Slowly entangling a web
of fellow homes :
So, I had come to the big one—
Well, bigger than I thought :
The library of lightning,
where my green blessed chakra
finally flew out its nest;
I had come to be part of a larger consciousness.

Had I really lost my way,
or was I truly in a healing place?

Moments of course
are fueled by intuition—
The type, for me,
where >> I see
depth within dimension.

I hear people lurking at me,
so at night,
I feel I have no ability
to sleep—

See, I took on the echo
a long, long time ago :
where I decided,
— I was. —
Then, The Breeze, I heard Her song,
*"People are mean to me,
in my reality;
there is something wrong
with my presence to seem—
wherever I go,
people either ignore or feed."*

As if a golden ticket
could not exist,
amongst a world
where people try to shoot and not miss.

I love myself,
so I took the effort to leave
my mind
and go out
to start it.

The Revolution,
May it be set!
—As I go inside my direction—
—of depth—

I speak from memories
accessed through liquid shine.
I speak through words,
one event at a time.

I ask myself,
*Where is the voice
that spoke to me through trees?*
I love myself,
For I am free—
I travel fro' my pyramid,
as my Sphinx
keeps [me] purring.

What'd You Find

4:36 in the morning,
Crack of dawning,
Losing track of jumpsuits
I'm donning.

To be pieces and the puzzle,
How perplexing,
To jump on in,
And live as blessing.

AĀBABEFĀBABGHỊCDČEFEAËFEGHÍ

Fruits from a tree,
Life steady falling — Floating to be Åir

Speaking from above,
Thus reach down — Grab my pencil
Recreation of edits — I learn to stencil

Untaught ways of moving magnetic stones,
Thoughts that are so stubborn — They hold their own

I've unlocked the passage,
To the chamber — so def
The 37th one — where you recapture your finesse.

Energy

Be the light
You wish to see in the world,
And see the light you wish to be.

Aquarius

I dream of you
in seas of blue,
Troubles flow out,
but filter through—
Your hands of time,
but who am I—
*To ask of you,
Such lovely truth?*

I hold the aspect
of sorrow at bay,
Disguising it with comfort
to my dismay—
Will I find the seer I seek?
Will we break
through the cowardice
of meek?

Scheme Free Rise

You are the judger
and the Lamb.
You are,
and I am!

The Portrait

The romance of the handsome cab
To live amongst the richest lands
With an intimate knowledge of the street,
Strap them down to fill the feat;
Out of hearts in the field,
Building seconds in reference to heal,
Stealing the book and saying hello;
Living on screen as if I know.

[Season 7, Episode 11]

Time doesn't exist in the 11th dimension.
— Bunny

8 on Tour, 11 on Shore

I stood inside a moment,
where people just walked by—
They ignored my presence,
as if I was in disguise—
I seek minds of reflection,
and tell of,
they rhyme.
I can feel through the music
that breaks up the distance
of quiet finds.

I am strong
and filled with force—
I awaken my insides
and ask them
to run their course.

I find myself in moments of truth,
when life swings over
and corrupts the vine.
Creates notion of relation
and altered states of Kind—
I trust in the humanity
of a Rainbow,
so few—
It becomes fluid to me,
and I,
furthermore,
manifest proof.

I am the White Rabbit,
The Vanilla you smell,
when you go to bed early,
as if a Band Aid could tell.

I am appreciative of Love
and all the Might it brings;
I am full of Love,
and I know it seems…
…like maybe so,
maybe not,
I resemble
a girl *all alone,*
or maybe a salmon,
who watched the 2000's
strip music chiefly to the bone.

I open my throat
filled with blue—
radiating the tribal sound
of all Truth,
as we observe Hope
get to be of knew.

I have so many friends,
and they all have a pH level
of '67—
so acidic;
they seem to be okay
with poetic mention.

I feel I am just;
I know I am full
of beauty and gust—
I unlock the Floor.

When I fall through the surface,
I find something dear,
a moment of dance—
a moment I dreamed of
so clear.

There is a dove that trails me,
and writes up my mind,
who creates synchronicity
then tells me, I am blind.
— a monkey on a string?
— or a blonde full of guilt?
what is the difference,
besides how society views
our skill?

But,
I step back,
For I manifest my own reality.
I am dignified in the way I walk
and seek true authenticity.
— — I, first, wanted a soul — —
another that could save me (from this Hell I concentrated),
but invisibility is a cloak of a wizard never traded.
I know my worth times three,
and I see you in perfect fallacy.
Supposedly, I died when I was 16,
therefore, this world I live in
will never control me.

I am strength;
I am lion to the bone.
I believe in Water reconciling
in waves of flow.
… I make a joke of myself — A Fool for the Sky
who wanted someone to admit to me
that my wings could expand and fly.
(The clones are getting closer),
I can feel the shadows growing opaque.
I put my intent into the fire,
and happy, happy I am
when I blow out that which conspires.

My senses are flared,
so, **CUE***,
it is — is
to adjust— —
my traction
to my inability
to rise above the morning's crust.
> *Stop!* < I remark
on the value of tries.
Possibilities are true,
but actions must be not,
because I get stuck in myself,
before removing my personality's rust.

I am Gold.
I am Copper.
I am Silver lining the barrel—
of a sword
that stops
with the ending
of the carousel.

They all laugh at me,
as they trot on by
and act like I am crazy,
just like Bertha,
who gave losing herself a try.

[I am a rose enthralled with theme]

FIXED SAND

Here nor there!!!
It holds no matter—

til it is changed into thoughtful pattern.

If I hold the spade,

then where is the joker?

I suppose the Earth is asking my card be turned over.
I jump with joy!
For She beats hearts within souls,

my manifestation comes forth—
to reveal all known.

As She renews roots

from the bread of my stones,
I gather strength

to finally turn over

the last unturned bone.

We'll call it *Earthism**

THE EXPERIMENT

Tearing up,
on the other side of truth
is a pragmatic distinction,
yelling,
"One of a Kind"—-

Tearing off my face,
Tearing off my spirit,
as I view through
control groups
to clear it.

TINKER
December 7th

Suffocated in a jar,
the fog pushes down on my limbs.
I become a tiny spec on the inside of your arm,
and a piece of art from within.
I don't see the past as holding any barriers,
since the water was stopped long ago,
but each waking day and each slumping night,
I see how far out seeds can blow.

A possible negative in my force field—
creates condensation on the glass,
A surrendered gesture of regret,
and, royally, a piece of the fast.

Walk! Free yourself!
Look amongst this Holy Land,
for indigo unveiling of the indigenous plan.

I stand here,
holding no ropes,
just the ones tangled up in my head.

I notice,
I am not separate,
from that which is my hand.

I can feel that—
It is ruthless; It is changing,
It is of nature to seek green.

—All is wonderful,
for allowing countless organic manifestations of one's dream.

Look around,
It's surround sound blasting all around the room.
It's kicking and screaming from Mother Nature's womb.
It's shaking my leg and looking into my eyes.
It's helping me into the car,
for a dream, a drive.
It's gliding up the stairs you make up for yourself;
It's holding onto my hair,
as I slip off the shelf.

It's forcing the voice so close to my ear,
and speaking words of *depardom*, as I fake a tear.
It's warm water rushing upon past attempts.
It's just another night.
It's as great as it gets.
It's waking in the morning,
holding up no signs.
It is worth it.
Is it worth it?
To be able to fly?

Shamanic Witch
to the akashic records!

Under lying tones,
Beating of drums, it sounds—
I've grown youthful,
but confused on most go theories,
ghost stories.

Medicinal Man

We join them in conversation

Awaken your senses,
and rise from your mind's deep trenches!
Reach toward the silver
and hold light and darkness,
as you shiver,
tune into a prop,
used senseless thing.
Transform towards a tree,
Eat, think, shrink !!
Hide your voice
below your confidence
in a box you dug up.
Realize that thyme could be different,
but I just … did … not plant … enough this … season …

Conversation carries on, as observer returns back home

IF

If you're waiting for the light,
then you've already missed the tunnel.
If you're struggling for the truth,
it's just self-breed denial.

I've never lost myself in a crowd
or inside a store—
I've just gotten mixed like a salad
& confused reflections with the door.

Perception is a prankster,
a trickster, if you will.
It acts as a movie,
but represents like a bill—
—causing inaction—
so governmentally insane.

We treat humans like mammals
& *label all and all,*—
"lol same"

"Look! A stable economy!"

FLIP MY SWITCH

Today's forecast calls for 3 Hail Marys
on repeat

It is mostly about me
and slightly about you.
If I could pick apart your brain,
then I would schedule us tea for two…

But, too, and through—
Alas! I want too much!
I wanted to pick apart your personality,
and then we could reminisce about it over next morning's brunch.

I move too quickly,
but slower than you know.
I tangle myself up in blizzards,
and I am looking for someone to get to know.

It is different out here,
when you've seen both sides.
I wanted love and peace to make sense,
but neither essence seems to coincide.

Happy is the new and spontaneous one I have found within the mountains;
A self that lives amongst sounds and a contention for passions.

At last! I feel hope again,
and I breathe fidelity into my lungs—
I am searching for completion, can you help me find some?

ANTIQUITY
Read your palm like a tree

I often ask myself,
How many pages are left?
In my book?
From my pen?

Are things to be different,
if they can't stay the same?

Past Barstow,
due West—
I lost track of the time.

I left my baggage on the carousel
& never looked behind,
because this race was for the big ones,
the ones with the cheese.

Passing on depth,
but dwelling on equality—
What's the difference to you?
What's the matter to me?

I feel neglected by a socio-ecological politician,
who claims to be the latest disc jockey—
To drop beats — instead of bombs,
—It would reek—
Hope from their eyes.

We would see humanity collect its belongings
& collectively redefine.

THE COMPANION
Oh, home! Out on the stage…

Excitement in verse

is all that is to be.

Life within a crucial effort

To push on til the dream.

If this is that, and I am so,

How do fractions of my ideas

arrive at destined home?

On the prairie,

And in the fields,

Are running redwoods

That I cop for feels,

And temptful in song

is the endeavor I hear,

So I keep on prancing

With the sound of dear.

KARMIC NAMES

"I lost my way,"

said the girl,

who was found TODAY.

CHANNEL 11, PARALLEL NEWS

I write for you,
in moments of time.
I fill in the mad lib,
& ad lib most theoretical finds—
I purchase a thesaurus,
So I can tell you,
all the ways thoughts pass over me,
in waves, of you.

I seek passages of *informity*,
to relish in the new—
of sweet, of current, of that which is true.

Of that which is root,
& that which is divine,
I seek the one
that which is thine.

TIGHTEN UP

I strive for beginnings
that remain in that realm of thought.
Introduction after Induction
after Deduction,
I am distraught.

It is quite typical
to wipe my lashes
and see my tears,
droplets of innocence shed from my heavy shoulders,
and suppressed,
are a series of years.

It is original to act out of
discomfort of the being;
in essence,
an existence turns to habit,
and I realize the simplicity
of my deviant believing.

Behaviors of flesh
and those who seek,
I am caught between gestures
of the grandiose and the meek.

When the dark of daylight
hits the lids of my eyes,
my pupils widen,
weeping in a pool
of defenseless cries.

If to be
was to want
and
to want
was to be,
when I look from glass windows
to projected glances,
I see and accept
that I am just a thing.

Systems of torture
and brackets of death,
I reach out for your body,
because it's the only hope I have left.

If I wanted to be told
of glamorous shortcomings,
then I would go to the riverbank
and dream about loving
...
somebody like you.
I do. I do.

Can you hear me?

Me vs. You vs. Me

Someday may not be an actual object,
but I will make it so,
Someday.

I used to do everything.
Now, I can count
the eyes that go by.
Love by love,
a condition unmet.
Can you try to remember?
If I try to forget?
-————-

Not aware of where
my minutes
will lead me to,
but I can always
find a
place to
lounge and something to
drink to.

Fact & Opinion vs. Advice

If you go crazy & don't write it down,
you'll be labeled insane, not a writer.

Mind's Maid Up

I urge you to clear the cobwebs of your mind.

——-··—-—·—-—··——

Describe your most vivid childhood memory—
Becoming friends with these girls down the street, who lived in a house surrounded
completely by prickly roses. *Hi, I'm Kendra. Do you want to play?* They were no
longer just the rose kids from down the way; they were now, my friends.

The Send Off

Layer, upon layer, upon layer,
Take these thoughts and construct her (on conveyer).
Make a mess of impostors
and liquidate the fragments with eraser.
Quickly, so quickly, drop the evidence,
hide the key and surround her!
Take the light, and take the room,
take the sunshine,
respond to fume;
open your mind,
and play with the time,
form a mould,
and watch yourself unfold.
Dribble the words on the interior of your head,
strangle the inferior,
and high-five the Fed.
Purge your cave
sunk behind your eyes,
whisper and echo,
hear red lies.
Watch them wail
as a band of scores,
View them switch and hand you the torch,
Scream your hearty bellows from below the water,
silence reckons as silence accompanies her.
Golden plates form from the skin of your thighs,
Tongues fly in from the loneliest skies,
the sun begins to set, as you sharpen your glares,
Bones cry out to the warning and the flares.
So, watch the blood drip, drip
from the pores of your alphabet,
and ask her to learn
to sincerely lead with accept.

60409

Staying up way too late,
A trick of the trade;
To the jester
gone hero,
aware
of display.

Howl,
one does,
at the aroma
of the roaming stars.

Glance,
one does,
at the shadowplay
of the clouds,
playing an ace
every card.

```
field notes:
  slanted poetry,
tales of drunken sound
```

{ 'Tis to be a flower,
and so exact.

Allowed to be alive
and filled with fact -

and once upon a theme,
I found -- the craft -

To be, To be, To be,
Softly found
on the brink

of budding endeavors,
whilst being two themes. }

WESTERN WORLD

How many spoons
in a row
does it take
to get what you know?
How many cares
are in a truth?
How many ideas
does one think
to fill up my booth?
Up and down
with resurrections

— And —

And around
the idea of
hollowed
Interjections.

*Welcome
to the gallery.*

Thanks.

MANIFEST DESTINY:
INSTANT MANIFESTATION NATION

I keep a crystal ball in my pocket—
for emergency purposes, you see…
For if I ever forgot it, it would seldom be beneficiary—
to any situation,
or circumstance of rhyme,
I do it to remember,
I'm never trapped in any single frequency of mind.
I fall upwards,
in silhouettes of mixtures of scented pine.
I burn leaves to warm the elder traditions of all shaped kind.

On a walk,
through my memory,
of a past lane,
I saw bumpers on the tracks,
helping me bowl a better game.

I thank myself quickly—
Well, thanking above, of course,
but sometimes, somehow,
I then generate the feeling of remorse…
For who am I to get a free pass from the hippy at the back door?
Lucky or greedy for setting up my own mental reward?

Hybrid Cars: A Paradox

SHARE YOUR SHOES

Awaken the Healer within . . .

Obsession,

Over a picture,

Of a soul

That could lighten the traveler,

And teach the code.

Of ethics,

Of morale,

And certainly, of point.

To co-create a habitat,

Silent within noise.

Near is the moment that calls from home

To cradle the spirit,

And love to the bone.

To be the power

Of electricity

That keeps me

in admirance,

That wakes

and soothes me.

RESERVATION(S):

Mind over matter,

matters to The Mind–

LIVE @

I'm in love with a day I've never seen.
I'm in love with a boy, a silly thing.
I'm in love with a thought that does not exist.
I'm in love with a feeling, a shot, a kiss.
I'm in love with the sun that does not shine.
I'm in love with the moon that brings the find.
I'm in love with the chase of your eyes—
Your smile, Your laugh becomes sublime.
I long for your words,
I long for your stance,
I long for every dawn,
A simple chance.
I long to be the light that gleams in your eyes,
or the standing grip that surfaces the highs.
I try to be right,
I try to bring dreams,
I try to be the Forever Girl
that causes the Beam.

PLATO'S STAR

Humans are all dust, which means matter is originally stone,
using the sun as a prism, the stars project themselves onto waking Earth.

#REGENERATION

We are told that we are the only hope for change to be seen in the world.
Then, we are told anyone who wants to be the change is acting like a little girl.

― ― ―

Drinking the cool-aid is fine, just be sure to bring your own jumpsuit.

― ― ―

The moment is within you before it begins.
— acting: the 1st six dimensions

THE PULLEY

Motions move through my skin
like sea bound repercussions.
—To obey who art within—

…

How to scribble the words of a madman speaking on point,
through mouths of recreation
& subjects of joint.

Shall be one to hold
& one to see,
Shall be one for the masses,
lightening the load for thee.
Where art thou in a pond of pity,
but under the miracle of a soul-bound lily?

To speak above the moment of own,
To learn to love the grace one's shown.
To be with thou everlasting soul,
To be & to sow of what I reap & console.

I call for your sweetness on nights like these,
when the seven days aren't passing,
& I'm no longer praying as a tease.

—All those seconds—

in-fact,
every single one—
I was playing
the dedicated role
of a sun.

I was & I am still shining right through,
all the lines I memorized
& related to you.

For friendship is just that,
a leaf to a tree,
the bound understanding that you need me—
& selfless it is for it glorifies infinitely.
To share your lightness & boundless energy,
I thank you for being grateful to me.

"All ashore that's going ashore."

The Grateful Lovers
they love each other

What is this name,
'tis on my lip?
You on barrel,
echo to 5,
You on redemption,
recollection of mine tribe.
Frantic to be,
I set down the clock,
who are you?
I remember that once now I had forgot.
Bless me with paintings
and hear me,
my words,
they come harrowing in
from the sunshine & life left absurd.

action

My Own [I'm Not There]

I didn't want to fall asleep in the middle of the late night morning.
It was bitter, it was cold, it was all yet warm.
I saw her leave her mark then cover it up with toasted embers.
She wanted it to be Fall again,
Winter woke soon.
She meandered round embrace again,
with her, spun symphonies of perfume.

"They down my lingo with heavy dropping of the jaws," She whispered,
"Chewing up agreement with the nomenclature of clause."

In decent exposure to radial dials, I watch her sit in silence,
with emotions running a river of rapid, I see her question the stride of valiance.
Integral to analogue, avid in the gratitude of presence,
a spiral of increasing steps to the faith of her's self-published.
She is notorious with familiars and wields her infinitives in oath,
Lounging on the right hand and offering lessons of Thoth.

She hooks her allegiance and lines her fate, sinking into the words she spells.
She wakes upon the crystal plane, as the Maya in Kali that dissolves.

Picking up the looking-glass, she makes herself peer into the mirror.
She thinks that she is inside that reflection,
yet I see it is me standing there.
I saw myself taking the pain,
but it was not me that was showing,
it was *her.*

Her triumphant happiness, her imagined exterior.

I saw her clear her eyes of crying and take a deep breath.
She smiled and began to fool them all again,
and I continued to help.

THE TRAVELER'S DIARY

On the way
to the top
is the slice
That is to say *stop*
And go!
Once again
From the walk alone,
Melting in stone,
Woodsy and playing loud;
In the grass,
Soundings of countdown.
This time in alphabetical order.
This time let's rock it in distortion.

As seen in your dreams.

- — — - — — - — — -

IT IS WINDY OUTSIDE THE CITY

Recalling your power in each breath you give,
stand in your compassion
& your heart will abundantly live.
Moments pass by as music to your ears,
so echo the sweet divinity
that you were born to hear.

On nights like these,
I think *what is it to be free*?
An abnormal response,
or a predetermined destiny?
I've been to the skirts of our lands of time,
and I've retraced many moments with the pupil of my eye.
So, I aim, now, to be above *that*...
[which is below myself too]
To reflect who one is *without a single clue.*

For who would be echoing a nation of sprouts,
but a hopeless minion made up to feel doubts?
I hear the buzzes as they talk to *we*,
Me is of one,
and you, I know, can see.

You've been here for hours,
days at a time—
You've seen past the production
of the falsely remarked twine.
The soul forms a spool of the fool I once knew,
Of the angel of death,
who wore black,
and saw blue—
but falling is floating,
if you remember kairological time,
if you recall the steadfast moments of trust,
when yourself knew it was inside your mind.
 — to the empaths I seek a redemption of sorts,
to help one another create foundation and not sport.
For I can hear you plotting,
which is me to myself,
to purposely lean in,
and thrive to develop.
The talkers are talking,
and the walkers are true,
to be waking up in life,
to see designs right through.

Peace,
Thank you

THE DEVIL'S ADVERTISEMENT

The light gives off darkness,
 just as my mind creates
  more adversity as it expands.

  The wick of the candle burns bright,
   as the essence begins to glow.
    At moment of spark…
     soon follows a descent into burning,
      and the orange and yellow flickering existence
      of life produces smoke that is
       as black as disappointment.

     May we not remain a melting candle,
      who disintegrates as soon as the
       light has begun.
        Let us remain not as
         an electric bulb either,
          soon to be jingling when
           shook back and forth.

        May we follow the sun and
         never fall asleep to the imaginable thought
          of breath without
           cognition.
            May I not be a source of allowance,
a tolerated light,
 for that which seeks to be extinguished.
  Instead,
   I ask to remain
    and retain
     our original orison of brightness.

ILLUMININE (9), NOT UNDERMINE

I am who I am. I will always be this. One cannot stifle the creativity of their mind's movement— nor shall I be distracted by a device made for machines, to make my eyes feel heavy & my knowing sound extreme. There is poison in my food and the air that I breathe. I am filled with toxins, yet cannot remember consenting? A rape of a culture or the colonization of a mind? I guess the grapes shall unfold, through the elasticity that is time.

Ever get the feeling that you are being sold back to yourself?

OCTOBER

Watch now,

Watch Free,

View me explode.

Tune in,

Turn out,

And prepare to reload.

Create space between your fingers and grasp for the group,

Don't mention the colors you obtain for proof.

Lie there, Lie still, Countless suspects foot the bill.

Running red, The negativity spreads,

The house becomes drenched in one, tiny threat.

A damper of laughs, A taker of scenes,

Close your eyes, Convert the team.

Behind your lids, View sets of the sun,

See running trees, searching for young.

Watch the blade create a little nic,

Bleed out your words til the community accepts;

Not old, not smart, not right, so you adjust,

Not creative, not electric, not perfect enough.

Now follow my lead and be conscious of things,

Slowly bow down and be fearful of kings.

Knelt at the bottom of the throne,

Give all your power to the forever unknown.

Nothing but a number, nothing but a tale,

Set your boundaries and get ready to scale,

The fence, the grass, the changing reflection,

The red, the blue, the desired correction;

Real eyes, realize, your unreal lies,

Now flip back and see nothing but hope,

Now accept what you are, to them your nothing but a joke.

If reality holds truth, I'd regret to admit,

Why play games with judgment? Nothing in return you'll get.
Now focus your line,

Now forget the time,

Listen here,
Listen now,
Stop acting for the crowd;
Be true,
Be right,
Expose your crown!
Find yourself where you left it in October,
Throw your arms in the air,

And realize it will never be over.

SIGN LANGUAGE

Everyone takes a dark turn.
This is why we follow the light.

We withstand growing in darkness,
yet thou who grows in darkness,
Well, ye es la luz(er).

THE CHRONICLES OF I DON'T CARE

The chronicles of I don't care
are something like this—
A scratch on the list
of ideals most wanted.

Skip, skip
one does
on down
the line
(fine)
to pick up
each rhythm
on all
of the time.

The chronicles of letting go
(I don't care)
are standing up
for what is
perfectly fair.

The Lullaby of Lady Liberty, nyc.

Encircled elbows tap on my windows,
cursing the day, I rose;
with a loaf of seasoned decapitation,
I eat up and spit out my foes.

"Why did you come here?"
he speaks from atop my shining torch.

"To create something," I sing,
"that buoys the gesture
of buyer's remorse."

*"But it's pumping through the country,
the doubt of palpable fear,
it's the gremlin that lies on your couch
pitching you conflicts you can subtlety hear,*

*and I know you'll give in,
in-fact I even bet.
They'll cast you to the water
as a frozen statue*

*and that's the best
you'll ever get."*

The Formular

Go slow,
Bite songs,
Don't give up,
Retreat when necessary,
Step out when possible,
Navigate the room,
Know who you are talking to.

If you are a revolutionary, just go for it.

Johnny Boy

"I haven't Written in
So long,"
She said.

"I haven't been here
Before," she assured.

"Shine on,"
He said
Then added on some other words.

It's me on the outside;
It's me from within.
It's me on the brink of
Understanding
Once again.

And I love
The way the sunshine
Picks up
When I step outside
To smoke.

He echoed in unison
"You crazy!"

        "You crazy what ??"

"You crazy
Diamond."

Aromatic

Retrograde is a hard hitter,
Giving up said life,
I'm not much of a quitter,
Roundabouts and ron de jambes,
Having to do with moving on.

Transmutation

I just entered a room Black with snow,
I just let go of your hand in a place I don't know,
I just forgot to look both ways before I cross the Road,
I just traded a smile for a heavy growing load,
I just opened the door for a stranger on the street,
I just opened the chances my mind will never meet,
I just watched the past and future exchange a simple greet,
I just touched the water with my land laden feet,
I just scratched the outer layer of a skin I've never felt,
I just shook hands with a choice I've never held,
I just watched my childhood run across the bridge,
I just watched my life through a pair of eyes
who have never lived!
I just grew into a statue speckled with Wise,
I just drowned a simple moment in a cupful of lies,
I just laid down the line to cross—
I just realized the severity of a loss,
I just stood up my thoughts
and showed them who's boss!
I just engulfed my head in a life I cannot toss,
I just looked up into the palms of a tiger,
I just succumbed and
never tried to fight her.
I just became a person who hast *truly* looked,
I just…
I just…

AROUND THE BODHI TREE,
Verses of A Mirror

Part one of me, myself, remembers past intention.
I receive what I am, and I sow of what is given.
Organically speaking, I shall ramble on through;
Pardon my bluntness, but the truth is not suddenly new.
Patterns of my speech mixed with the use of specific conjunctions--
Hell! If it were 1942, I'd reap a paragraph of repercussions!
Sentenced to writing a dialogue with no lines,
the text we speak in conversation reflects the subtext of our daily lives.

ENCOUNTERS

I write to release the past
I assume is me—
I write to recover false
descriptions of integrity.

Shall I embarrass myself
by being to be—
or underwrite the script
that my actions
perceive?

I am Kendra,

& this is so——

I bellow it deeply

& repeat costumes from my drawer.

My well of emotions

is from the whole of my control—

I find it odd to label

what is not of one's own—

Then why do I claim the words

as mine known—

when in actuality it

is from the glitches I am shown.

I create constructions of thou,

who mightest be me,

but then complain

when that mightiest version

is my highness beyond eternity—

For why beckon for credit

when thou art the living truth—

The waking monuments of ancient swimmers

reincarnating into youth—

& co-existing through contract:

We are the cast of Godspells,

Who signed up for the act.

With me,
Remember:

The precious calls we received,

while waiting in the wings

for our cue to believe.

Remember:

Our shared glances backstage,

when the director was our Father,

& our mind was the page.

To be in agreement,

to flow,

yes,

from the bowl of healing

sounds and returning

scenes of our home.

To be of agreement and free-will

in one—

To act from singular motive,

while also dancing for fun…

Touch of

Strength of a past——
Year to year,
Hopes for a path,
A chance, a fear,
Step towards a bill that costs more than put forth,
Strides to a chase and a chase to a force.

Grasps for blank white,
A beginning ensues,
Threads that break barriers,
Feelings seem true,
Thoughts tumble to a whisper,
A fool to follow through.

Thoughts turn into knots,
Knowing became knew.
Judgements become pastimes [past times],
Viewed through a mirror,
Bones become frigid,
Fists all you hear.

Pores start to drip,
and fall slightly towards the near.
Near morphs into far,
and your mind swims in a tear.

The rivers start flowing at a speed nobody should crave,
HAPPY BECOMES FRIENDS WITH LOATHING,
and stakes a hideout behind your face.

Truth begins dripping down the throat of a Knight,
Lies born twins with sayings,
All moments ignite!

Math builds a castle,
Strings to build a moat,
Geometric sigils to blow away and slide slyly down his throat.

The King becomes engulfed in a plagued war with time,
Minutes slice to hours,
and hours are cut with choice,

The Winter numbs your head,
Followed by a thoughtless little voice.

You begin to shrink to the bystander that you are,
Pain is held captive behind a pen;

Follow far!

The gold loses its luster,
and the diamonds revert to coal;
you become molded [moulded],
by the moments you hold.

Plato brain…
Play-doh brain?

I See You [The College Essay]

As the saline slides down the clear tube, I lay there viewing the bystanders through a glass pair of eyes. A world that used to stand on its own has now been reverted to crawling. I gasp for air in an atmosphere new to me. With each lift of my eyelids, I see the people, I hear the voices, and I taste the dry space consuming my throat. My mind searches for the words running around in my mouth, only to pull out simple responses and gaps between each question that the unknown lady presents to me. The date slips my thoughts along with the time, and hours seem to bend into seconds. The current happenings are handed to me without my consent, as necessary oxygen is gifted by necessity.

Fate begins to blur with the six doctors surrounding me, and nurses begin to dance with needles to solve my case. My pain seems to slip out the door along with my fearfulness, and I watch as the two wait til I can assess the situation. One-day earlier, I was empty of IVs and empty of medicine. Although I slowly became empty of health, that one-day prior to entering the hospital, I still held choice.

As I lay, outstretched in confusion, I stare at the tubes connected to my once loose wrists. I feel the pull of the strings; like a puppet, controlled by hands, my future was in the palms of another person. In those moments of desperation, my trust had nowhere to hide. My mind had nowhere to run and crouch in the shadows. I found my life rounding the corner of something new. I began to realize that my next steps were in the hands of people I did not know, and before my mind could understand the letters 'ER', my point of view encountered significance.

Throughout the journey of defeating the Swine Flu and Pneumonia, I began to see my daily activities in a new light. I began to feel the burn of maturity rising from my toes. As it slowly crept up my legs, the clock never stopped; time proceeded to saunter by. While my health became dependent on the trickle of antibiotics down the bag connected to my roots, I lay there holding no choice and no ability to make my own decisions. The playground of thoughts and words in my head became my only freedom. Only there could I escape and run among the lush, cushioned walls of my hopes.

As I defeated my illness, I was transported into facing reality. I became aware of the fragility of life, and I began to appreciate the simple sunrise I watched as my blood was taken early each morning. I recall when my mind took the leap from child to adult. A haze of medicine and doctors, I found myself finding comfort in closing my eyes. When I closed my eyes, I could walk around my dreams, and I could forget that my lungs were depending on a machine to feed me air. My first memory of the hospital began when my eyelids were sealed. I felt my soul as it looked at my body. I felt my soul as it darted around the room. In my dream, I felt the emptiness of my organs as my soul rose above my body and looked down at past mistakes of mine. In a flash of realization, I felt my chest muscles cramp as my body arched forward, and my soul darted back in. Awoken with gasps for breath, my thoughts began to walk towards a new perspective. I watched as fate walked down the tip of my nose, and I realized each moment is a blessing. I realized life is about the present, not about the past.

Go Waves!

The Salivation

Lips are unseasoned with ones I have seen,
They've become pale to the bones,
and false to the teeth.
They flash their presentation
with the glances of a fiend,
Grazing current looks,
with lies — they stay keen.

"Formation!" I yell,
from my gutted brain's hope,
Privation to control with light,
I've seen oaths.

Neglect of unsighted
and brought up with despair.
I've stood facing their emotions,
as you touch the face of fair.

I've seen,
I've been,
I've constructed my nails;
not a subject to toy with,
I hold the mention of my own grail.
I'm forecasting my eyes on the only one I knew,
I'm leaving the past
with birds,
I flew.

I'm pulsing with words
and etching with consonants;
I'm mad to the eyes,
I'm eating up nonsense.

"Stand here and look straight into the light,
Look! Look around! Not an enemy in sight!
… And then CHOP ! I chop off their heads."

Jams, Pt. I

Frontwards to a plain [plane],
filled with sight and sound,
back into a deception of
muddled letters and ticking numbers—
traverse all that's found.

Connection to my fingers,
running after light,
Commitment to my eyelashes,
what I won't see will not
reach and bite.

Surrounded by a sea that later turned to grey,
Construction of a plea
to make my ears friends
with betray.

Perception turns to distance
as you recline my thoughts,
Interception of built up lies,
all circles turn to knots.

Jumble of straight barriers
and weights added to my eyes,
Hope thrown to Ashes,
Love partnered to try.

Past built to crumble,
Time built to hold,
Bones built to protect her,
Moments built two fold,
Words form to letters
and letters set to convince,
I hold all the time,
but you hold all my sense!
Go! Give me a memory!
Give me a thought!
Give me my oxygen,
My choice turns to Walk.

THE SUN GREETS THE MOON
Where are you?

The gift of a God

Or the bud born to Rose?

From the ashes

Of Herself,

Together, She chose;

To be of Love,

To be open to Source,

To hug her companion

On this Saturday course.

When life loops in rhythm,

The Sour joins The Sweet,

To convene in attraction

And walk over to Her feet.

An ease basks Her toes,

And rises Her soul to the occasion

of hearing

Her lover greet.

And we know,

The story to unfold,

Has bloomed underneath,

The glow of The Moon

Held in The Sun's reach.

Love to

Kendra,

Fed from

Belief.

Thanksgiving Eve 2009
flashes of mk

I've been created by a monster,
 Who withdrew from my head,
  I've been lured in by a chance
   of being the ruler of all said.
    Consumed by a moment,
    Consumed by a word,
   Letting consciousness drip
  to an ending,
Saturating all I heard,
 Filling the tub
  with a feeling of regret,
   Reversing my mind,
    Control, I forget.
    Leaning towards a memory
   in the distance, trains.
   Evoking detachment,
 I make room for my brain.
  Glowing with senses,
   I lost what I knew,
    I became a person filled
     with interruptions,
    and over my body,
   My soul flew.
 As my lungs fill with realization,
and my choices meet Sir Time,
 My eyelids slip to slumber,
  As my dreams follow its rhyme.
   Before now and until then,
   I was drowning in the past,
  I was playing pretend with symbols
in seconds that surely (never) last.

Pendulum

And I ask myself, "why 'tis so difficult?"
    To be the wind and also the lightning bolt.
        And so, I endeavor the being of said now,
            Bowing and succumbing
                to the idea of profound.
                      Once up on the bridle of thee,
                unseat didn't idea of a dream;
        I founded the dousing,
            I am the feeling—
                I am the terrible story—
                    that is giving and
                          receiving.
                              - -
                             -

TRILL

She has a heavy fucking Frito Lay
on her shoulder,
Some call it a chip,
I call it hierarchal structure,
Tell me (x2)

So, what's this generation all about?
A generation of me, he,
or just a damn selfie.

I was on my way out,
as the lotted hands tried
to muffle my mouth.
You know,
down South,
some say *though*,
you can catch me riding glossy
in my Lincoln 4 door.

So, watch with me,
in 3D…
As I drop the track
"We're Founding".

Once more,
I gather up my nonsense,
and call it Suess,
the same doctor
who is trying
to prescribe me some weird tasting juice—
And gave me this order,
to respect all kinds,
'cause those who
disregard
don't matter
of mind.

If I were a creature
of fright,
then I'd pick on you,
but I only came to dance!
And I came back to Texas
just to bang Screw.

If I was Mo City,
or even Don Ke,
I'd still rap about
my white ass homies, you see…

They were there the OG time
I ever heard——
talkers conspiring
to move my inspiration
from a suburban to a hearse.

I had all these problems,
Not knowing which one to solve,
so, casually, I'd
drop a ladder
in my bubbly
and watch it dissolve.

RIP PIMP C

Adjacent to Black Top

Speaking words
to rhymes
is real swift,
Floating up
and down,
as I shapeshift.

Looking for actions
of severe improvement,
sorting motions out,
as I choose them—

Waiting on the soil
of a new stone,
resting, ultimately,
on an unknown—

Understanding
of root
and being.

Loving and
giftful
for the speak
that is blessing.

1 & 2 x 4 + 1 >> 1 & 2

I spend hazy time alone,
Real quick,
I run mansions through your mind,
Over with.

I'm speaking words so blunt—
My friends often smoke it.

Arpeggios

Tuned tension to feel what is felt,
Float drips pain,
Full metal mountain,
Rooted in spring,
Up flows the motion that electric natives bring.

The occasion is coarse,
but also a symbolic gesture;
To be,
To be of bone and still to muster
Up the energy one needs.

Suspension of dimension[al plots],
Untangle[d],
Moma's dance under thoughts.

Circles,
Clear,
Clarification of control,
Clouds in the distance,
Speak of once told.

Unmarked pages,
Blank,
Bare,
Barely,
Beacon of Beckoning,
The circles got me up,
So I stopped smoking [squares].

Ekphrastic
inspired by PH 435; 1935 - Clyfford Still.

Melted face
like something I stole
and made with the tithing,
a helm below stone.

It rolls on me
and looses my guts,
spills my beans
and picks at my lunch.

It packs like a rat,
my shoulders, its home,
I shrug it off,
the sadness of a hunch
I condone.

Permissively,
I, the machine,
casts the lyrics
it loans to me.

My fingers,
they stretch
to hold their own.

This woman
to my left,
is made of bone.

Ekphrastic, II.
inspired by PH 247; 1951 - Clyfford Still.

Across from me,
I see shades of brown,
I question if they are feathers
or the blood of a massacred town?

Was it a village?
Was it a society?
Oh, LORD, my GOD,
is this the origin
of my anxiety?

Ekphrastic, III.
inspired by PH 1074; 1956 - 59 - Clyfford Still.

What comes to me
is a fragment,
A fly I see
face to face.

A speckle of illusion
turns as gravity
spinning reality
into this space.

Making of light shine
reflecting the timed
barrel of a tunnel.

To see one as
paint (everywhere)
dripping,
coating the
telescope I channel.

My breathing in comfort,
I feel a push away.

A winged creature
choosing to roam
throughout day.

Meeting as agreement,
inverting a tale on display,
or always together ? —
I hear they wanted it
this way.

33333

In all directions,
Like two first names,
We fold like boxes,
Calling in controlled expansion.

Master of the ring,
too old fashioned.

The blessing is in your court,
Bovine Goddess.

Sugar

What would it be - -
to turn to another page—
Where I held no more concept,
Where I saw no more stage?

It would be a new state
of forgotten words,
where we looked at each other
and beheld the observed.

So beautiful,
So linear,
and so out of line,
Where time regains value,
and life redeems mind.

Synchronistic is ALL,
VAST within SMALL.

Healing my vine,
as I gaze past seen scenic venues
and phenomenas of humankind.

It's magic,
It's *Linguatic*,
It's seeking the love—
   —of a light-solar being,
   who has legs

   and blessedly walked,

   purposefully,

   into my dream.

   [To wake me]

Stories

He walked into the room,
and the allegory within her
awoke.

[Karmic] Jams, Pt. II

Dripping from the barriers
of seconds inspected with tries,
Building from the letters of sounds
that dance around with lies.

Moments float to femurs
and femurs climb the trees,
Mothers spinning words
in quote
to suffocate *dis ease*.

Eyelashes depart from
the spot set to live,
Legs grow upon them
and the Humans begin to give.

They place weights on my eyelids
and force down my sight,
They place air in my thoughts
and make me gasp for
a melee filled fight.

Confusion takes the place
where constructors labeled *breathe*,
They took smiles from my vault
and surrendered my mouth
to grieve.

They put thoughts in my blood
and fed my ears lies.
They put hours on my clock of
all events grown to despise.

They cracked open my shell
and filled me with Hate.
They hollowed out my soul
and iced me with given traits.

They surrounded my throat with
hands of help,
but help runs to shadows
when Truth gets up off the shelf.

Consciousness slowly peeks out my nose,
as They begin to sing hymns of love
and hymns filled with mind melting creeds.

It steps out to the light and
dives in too low.
It opens up my follicles
plastered with scripted foes.

Ice grips the feet of a Summer approaching.
White melts to past times [pastimes],
as you use me and dispose of…

Plans talk to children,
of them I can't see,
Hands talk to mouths
of a life set free!

Written with the tips of your knuckle,
You begin to believe,
but frames turn to edits,
and I watch as your actions
make my thinking succeed.

When words begin to fumble,
and seconds don't make sense,
I realize Time has handed me moments
to reverse that I exist,
I stand as I stumble
and I march as I walk,
because I need an answer to my solution
and you forgot to knock!

SPOKEN TRUISM

"The dream falls in heavy
on the brink of an early rising moon.
The day,
soaked in envy
for a child
fed glory
by a spoon.
Feeling and open
and certain to be,
All around the subject,
yet the subject is me.

Tracing the glances,
And teaching my rhymes,
To lick the desire of floating," admits Time.

5

I could love anything about you.

If you told me to,
I could love your eyes.
If you told me to,
I could love your smile.

If you grabbed my hand,
I'd squeeze back.
I could fall in love with disaster,
If you whispered in my ear that it was good.

I could learn to chase the sunshine with flower petals,
If you told me it was beautiful.
I could learn to love life and just plain day,
— wrapped in your gaze.

I could stand up against my fears,
If you told me I would win.
I could rub my tears out with your sleeve
And hear your heartbeat
When mine was froze.

I could learn to stand confident,
If you told me you'd stand with me.

I could love you forever,
If you loved me too,
or I could forget about us,
Just like you.

Sigh bore, hack ...

Freedom.
Oh, to be
and then some!
Okay,
Okay,
Okay,
I see
believe
idea
of a drama…

…Book,

ideas of what I shook.

I crate
and rock
and roll
is what I speak through.
Peace on the presuppose
of…
…of

" ID, please! "

        " Please, can I send you FB ID. "

" Sadness! "

        " Confirm. "

12/12/13

Pen,
Paper,
and
Tomorrow.

　　　　　　　　　Pencil or pen,
　　　　　　　　　Paper or skin,
　　　　　　　　　I'll write it down,
　　　　　　　　　　　　or else,
　　　　　　　　　　　I'll forget.

Tell Me About You
　　　　　　　You seem really specific,
　　　　　　　Interesting to say the least.

　　　　When I get caught up in movements,
　　　　I recall the stillness of your speech.

　　　　　　　　　Must I keep writing,
　　　　　　　　or should I end it now?
　　　　— Because days are getting longer,
　　　　Yet I still keep moving, somehow.

House, Keeping
Everything was fine,
but there was nothing to do.
I was stagnant for too long.
I was lost inside you.

　　　　　　　　　　Breakdown to rebuild.
　　　　　　　　　　Redesign to respond.

The Synchronicity

I shall pass on the good news,
I discuss it further with those who already knew,
Aware of the void my ego carries into the room,
I cut up fearful talkers,
The ones who speak from low mood.

Only concerned
of reasons not to be,
I flip and see—
      I am holding true love,
My soul speaks
      And beams
         That of above.

                As well as,
            Through and True.

    {Of course,
You are a creator.}

New Age Wasteland: Papa… oh, really?

New Age Wasteland immediately draws our attention back to who?
The Who!
Swinging their instruments around,
as if they invented gravity.
They bring in a sense of balance [to a certain extent]
that provides both the yin & the yang—
Yin being the feeling of not giving a fuck
by means of full self-expression on stage [and in lyrics].
As well as, the yang that holds the powerful essence
that is that of commitment to rock 'n roll & it's mission…

Inspiration is the theme of a place.

—.—.—.—.—

Mac & Wood

The Muse,
She burns so bright.

*Vocalizes the peaces,
(Sings) of poetry*

—.—.—.—.—

The Vision

Steep along the mountain hill,
are gorgeous sunflowers,
I water for frills.

—.—.—.—.—

To be —
is a verb,
an ongoing event,
but also, a choice.

Groovin' to arise to movement!

COPPER GOLD

There walks a girl...

Write a poem,

They say,

They say;

I pick up my pencil,

To their dismay.

Is she following orders?

How out of whack!

For this girl to follow rules,

Would show a sign of contact.

Ground control to major Tom,

Ground control is having fun.

Ground control is into it,

Ground control ain't telling shit.

NEXT-PIONAGE

Rocking the book,
and burning old ideals,
Over-standing values,
in reference, to heal.

MAGNA CARTA
An ode to Venice Beach

I am here,
I am Alice,

A vision of a tear.

That is alive,
That is vacant of fear.

I am you,
I am me.

I am all repercussive,
Not a theme.

I am real,
Not to be discussive.

———

To be,
To not,

To know the plot.

To live,
To breathe,

To trail in everything.

To be what one says,
How wouldn't thou be denying,

To live,
To breathe;

I am self aligning.

THE CITY FOR MILES

My favorite thing about Denver
is the way the sunshine picks up my smile.
On the route of description,
I found myself heading East
to love a girl who is myself.

She was covered in definitions
she created for play,
and now, in The Mile High City,
she was pulling it off.

She came here
for soul searching,
and here she saw
her findings
were the grains of truth
she had always known,
yet waited
for the mountains
to uncover.

From the sand
that was her mind
dancing in the breeze,
she linked together
unskeptical pluralities
to make point,
to make art,
to make sense
of choosing life
with heart.

A PEACEFUL TREATY
no need for an alter ego,
let that go,
no longer is defining a limitation.

THE GILL OF

Summer of Love (1968)

I own no TV,
Yet, I am an image.

I have resourceful thinking,

Yet, I scoured the pilgrimage

For a redundant meaning of a text

Of holy misunderstandings

Of seldom held belief

and known reprimandings.

I speak from a tablet of a bird

With a mind,

Which is quite absurd.

I sail on through the storm

and guide the lightning to its shore.

I reconvene with myself.

I am a fish

On tour.

FLOWERETTE

Artlessness,
it remains at the beginning of the road,
with aspirations of hope,
making me reach further,
my small arm could extend;
The concoctions engraved in my young mind
were potions resulting in different fates.
Everything began to brighten,
my needs dwindled to that of a picturesque thread,
and conversating got filed away as means to evidence.

Priorities changed with the seasons,
and at times, isolation became easier than words.

. . .

SUNNY STAND

Nights like these
appear and go,
Nights as if my mind is eager
to counter flow,
I am sinking into
the understanding
much faster.
However,
moments
and energy often
stagnate in matter—
If I were to be gazing
on such that
is this disaster,
I'd tread around
stuck in two
guesses.

where does this everlasting feeling stem from?

—·—·—·—·—

AND STILL

There is a tale
About a King
Who made a castle
To fulfill His Queen.
There is a tale
That starts like this.
In the beginning,
She was scared of kids.

RELATION5SHIP

We call it poetry,
We call it farce,
We call it Love
floating around distant givers
in bars.
We pick up the call,
We pick up the tab,
We call it connection, because,
Baby, that is all that we have.

EARS UP

A guest is a person you meet on the way,
To the epicenter of gifts on display,
A person is a blessing,
A creed of its word,
A being is a person,
Born to be heard.

SWEET LOVE

Soundly…
I watch myself pace around.
I teach myself peace through moments profound.
It took me a few moments of locating clouds,
To realize the shadow is truly my light bound—
To the context of script in hand,
Do the obvious,
Rationale without plan.
When I land over the moon,
in ecstatic joy,
I release the sun
From thoughts that annoy—
I'd like a dinner date
with my heart-lead boy.

WHO IS HE?

He is everyday with the wind and the space of my thoughts,
dancing round barriers of enchanted storytelling,
watching our names burn through the page as fire.
He is the whisper of silence in my mind
that graces my ears with melody; He is & I am.

THE NIGHT CAP

Beauty was everywhere,
It was everywhere I looked,
It was everything—
moving, pulsing, swaying
further then back again
and again,
and again,
and again…

And the old couple turned off the lights,
Sailing off to sea in the morning.
It was usual,
regularity
at its best.

And I felt good.
Melty like cheese.

THE POWER GRID
Broadcasting from a mental agenda near you!

Somedays come & go,
without pointing to the next,
so,
I huddle down low,
& break at the crest——

A waveform of a person
[a being I love]
——To me, is so beautiful,
I shall repeat so for the above.

To be so sweet,
all of divine,
blossoms forth from boulders,
& fractals,
as it defines.

Oh, Justice!
To come out & play!
For the piper to attend,
then lead us the way.

Since millimeters are separating
the conscious connection
we know to be true,
I turn into a deer.

*Dear,
I am not blinded by the light,
are you?*

Golden surfaces,
glazed into 20 moulds,
3 detailed maps a plenty–
I count the fingers on my toes.

I scribble on the clock of testamented time,
Where I use nonsense
to avoid
writing
a single
emotional line.

- — - — - — -

*Up all night just to think,
what do you think about that?*

34 '09 15 YEARS

Imploding the surface,
Scratching the seas,
Hold my hand,
yet set me free.

Open my palm,
and read my mind,
Caress my head,
become only mine.

Be a thought,
Be a character,
Be a villain,
Then chase after her.

Hold her down,
and feed her bread,
nutritious and right,
She slowly loves The Dead.

She sheds her skin
and creates a new,
Grabs pieces from others,
If only they knew.

She traces their steps,
She traces their words,
She becomes a follower
along with the birds.

She jumps the gap
and fastens the bridge,
She outsteps the trap,
yet jumps off the ledge.

She free falls towards the destine
and becomes the Dredge,
The *stop* and *stops,*
The straight becomes the edge.

So record the tape,
and create brief space,
lead my body into the gate.

I've become a victim,
says the Angel Gabriel.

I've become a criminal
locked in a cell.

Stop the foolish
and *stop* the tale,
Look in my eyes,
I'm learning to scale!

THE FOURTH GOSPEL

I pace round and round.
I circle around your bed.
Your bones linger in my memory
and taunt the suppressions within my head.

I told you to leave me be
and let me live alone.
But now, I am all alone,
with no one to save.
You creep amongst my nightmares
— Attempts to keep me in place —

You commanded me to remain,
Prone was I,
To seek a solution,
that was not to find.

I will circle around the necks
of those culturally martyred.
I will be the haughty pig
within the pin to be slaughtered.

I am nodding off to sleep,
I am thinking of you.
Your ribs are but a mistake,
only Eve and I knew.

- — — — - — — — -

I wish people knew—
the person behind the eye
was never created
to become a freckle
of their past.

February 11

I am youth [x1]
I am health [x4]
I am love,
I am wealth,
I share my offerings
with community as self.
I am clever,
I am stealth.

Together, we stand.
Together, we evolve.
Together, we collectively
get to know God.

— - — - — - — - —

Diablo Blanco

Slipping doesn't matter
under castles made
of grandiose materials.
It files away like paper emotions,
ink bleeding on spilled
supposed
criteria.

If good is a god I've never known
then what is another hour alone?

Slipping doesn't rather happen
from charismatic gestures,
Slipping under measures
of measures
of simplistic solemn
sleepers.

Tears of Joy

Tears of recognition
Like tears of joy
Rock 'n roll
My soul
And show me my ploys

As I stand when I fall
I re-originate my direction
In flashbacks of blues
That flash on the screen
Like correction

Tears of joy
Like noise
Coat my bones in roses
And fill my tub with koi

They swim past my feet
And chomp on my toes
Until I commit
To the toast of the code

Tears of reconciliation
Like tears of joy
Sing to my grandfather,
The mountain I climb,
To search and destroy

Tears of sadness
Like tears she cried
To brighten the other
And hunt the find

She's pulling herself up
Up out of the water
She thanks the trees
For the solemn melodies
They give her

Tears of recognition
Like tears of joy
Rock 'n roll
My soul

WHOOOO ARE YOU?

*Oh, to be Alice **and** The White Rabbit, Chasing oneself!*

Underground is the sport that gives,

the game the name of reporting shives.

Above the trance of forlorn eyes

is the foam that must choice in disguise.

Thank you in all,

and thank you in essence.

Be the Rose that releases temptations,

To sing and dance on the blood of rounds,

Smile and type the shake of mornings profound.

We join in 3s and leave by 4s,

We open the perception

in the following ship of doors.

Yonder, I call in bones that fall,

From the rotund conjunction,

From the human walking tall.

Luma Sunset

I keep closing my eyes,
and I keep them closed.
I lie awake under lids of flesh.

Lay my head down to sleep,
My eyes' mind is tired,
and my maid still needs to sweep!

- - -

Honey and Oatmeal

One to remember,
and in the wake of that,
Let us remember,
To not forget.

- - -

Mannequin

Her to him,
is me to you.
Him to me,
I suppose we are through.

- - -

Optional

It disappeared when I called your name. I cried out for a junior cheeseburger,
you called me insane. So, I stopped in my tracks, and I withdrew myself.
I could see through your lame mysteries and attempt at stealth.

— - - — - — - - —

3:31 am

In equality, the sum of our parts is equal.
In equality, we see we are the sum of all total.

time x space

Phantom, Pt. III

I woke up from the dream-boat,
The one that held only me and you,
But when I woke up,
I did not wake up next to revelation,
Nor did I wake up to you.

I was asleep in a bed,
disguised as a casket.
It was filled with my lame attempts
to stay grounded——

And when I finally awoke,
You had thithered once more.
I found that I had been stripped of dignity's aspects.
I had been reduced to a silly bore.

I was deep in a sleep that required two.

You left me to swim
back to the shore,
Where earlier,
together, we made promises,
To never *stop* searching
til we discovered more.
But you misplaced me in the crosses,
not even polite enough to yell, *"Fore!"*

We did not think to bring reality,
And we did not remember to bring sight;
We wanted to find the purpose,
But I guess one decided on fright (basically).

And so I awoke, my lungs gasping for air!
Looking within me,
I saw nothing,
But dust and guitars.

Forgive me, please !!

I love you.
I wish you knew,
The way the birds pass the ocean blue.

The way you view from atop,
The way you sense and sense and *stop*.

I wish the sun aligned with me;
I wish the moon would shine and be!

I hold the hope of a life a free.
You hold the call of worship,
Prospects from a tree.

I wish you could understand the beckon of my cries.
I wish you could reprimand
my trials and my tries.
I hope someday you'll hold my hand in yours.
I hope one day
you forgive past attempts and closed doors.

The Horizon is to brighten,
and The Soul is to find;
I began to rustle,
and you began to fly.

Yes, I am just a kid,
and I might be a thing,
but I am not just so ignorant,
Not a stupid, helpless fling.

I blossom with the leaves
and play with the flowers.

I team up with friends
and successfully jam for hours and hours.

I am a production,
but not just a scene.

I am a tradition;
I've began to seek the decree.

I'd like to talk with the lipless
and play Mississippi in Half-Time;
I'd like to go back to the moments
where it was only you and I.

See this as forgiveness,
Served amongst a circle plate,
See this as justice,
An end to projected hate.

I love you,
I mean it
in words,
but more in thought.
I love you,
I live it
in worlds,
even after we have fought.

— Karmic response let rest —

Moontribe

Everyone will outcast you,
if you allow the will—
You must be patient—
However, how is <u>what</u>
real?

In rite (I write),
Poetry and Care.

———

There used to be fun in this.
Ah, yes, the one with all the stories!
No one wanted a damn thing to do with me!

———

I had forgotten my makeup bag,
barefaced to the crowd,
What an outcast.
Yet the signs were all the same,
I decided to cut all the factors
that I thought mattered,
so I could live sane.

How could I write
so limp in the hand?
Oh, Spirit, Great Spirit,
H Hawk soars.

———

I am for what is thee
but something I know.
Why not treat all like summer camp,
You plant what you grow—
because I am a bargain;
I tell you upfront,
What I am and
What I am <u>not</u>—
<u>still</u>, you grunt.

> yawn <

Degeneration Nation

I'm sitting on the table.
I'm sitting outside your door.
I'm becoming who I said I would not,
Seeking attention more and more.

I promise I will be different,
as I really just stay the same.
I promise I'll be better,
as I continue to feed my brain.

Baskets full of cases,
and heads full of dead,
I remark on your appearance,
but nothing was actually said.

I wrote down my thoughts,
inside the lids of my eyes.
I wrote down my circumstances,
once chosen to despise.

I am slipping away further,
and faster than before;
I'll be your little angel,
Your little attention whore.

> actors <

Found Electricity

I found myself here
in a place I can't be.
I can't stand the creaking walls
or the endorsement of phalanges.
The district of contortion,
leading thoughts away.
feelin' bad.

It is right here lying
next to me in bed.
It is whispering to me,
encouraging the joint of hands.

Telling me to think about the fabric of demands.

It keeps shifting in its chair
and begging for my attention.
Itching her head to understand my mind
and its conviction.
She is grasping for my sight
with each word of her lungs.
She is bracing my bones
in efforts of remaining young.

She is conducting processes
of improvement each day, each rise.
Along with the clouds,
She stares straight through my disguise.

She holds a mask—
in her bony, moving fingers.
She only brings it out
when a moment decidedly lingers.

I let her soak me
in her desperation
for desire—
She drowns me in attempts
as I disintegrate to a liar.

She traces my spine
with her pupils
and constant structure.
She is Death,
She is Power,
I must grow to trust her.

Her eyes lodge my brain into
a room of doors I lock.
Ones I allow her to open,
and other times, I make her knock.

I raise up my voice,
just loud enough she can hear;
I can only find that
girl's eyes
when I am looking
in the mirror.

———
—.

A Sheep in Wolf's Clothing

2 people sitting on opposite sides of the stage, facing the audience. They are unaware of each other's existence. Mood is sullen, contemplative. Person 1 has gusto of a 'wolf'. Person 2 gives off the air of a 'sheep'. (The people are actually the 'same' person. Person 1 is the appearance, the way the person is viewed by society. Person 2 is the personality, the truth of self in the face of society.)

Person 1: This is what they see.

          Person 2: This is what they overlook.

1: How I have become a cloud.

          2: How smiles cover what concrete took.

1: When waters have grown silent.

          2: When charcoal sullies white.

1: Why thoughts are traced with mirrors.

          2: Why my mind can't get out to fight.

1: What carries the sound of distance?

          2: What carries the sound of remorse?

1: What changes the meaning of vision?

          2: What they see is judgement's force.

1: Could the truth be buried deep beneath my surface?

          2: Could I be seen as a different character simply for that purpose?

1: Does the strength of my voice matter?

          2: Does society view only what they see?

1: How could assumptions be made from my appearance, when this is truly...

2: Me?

1: Is the shepherd away? Has he vanished, in-fact?

2: Is the depth of my skin all that is lacked?

1: Can the past be incorrect? Something doesn't fit.

2: Can the past be searching for someone who only appears perfect?

1: Should I stand for these eyes?

2: Should I stand from my chair?
(stands from chair)

1: When dodging generalizations seems impossible.

2: When dodging illusions leads me to despair.

1: What happens when the herd has left me as I am?
(stands up)

2: What happens when the herd has let go of my hand?

1: Where is the author? For he got it all wrong!

2: Where is my chance? It's been too long!

1: Why am I all they see? For I am just the outer person.

2: Why am I locked in this head? Can't you see we're the same person?

1: How can I make them see that there has been a mix up in thoughts?

2: How can I make them hear that their view is in a restrictive box?

1: Now step back and see, I am not truly the beast you've been loathing.

2: Now step back and see, I'm simply a sheep in wolf's clothing.

About Time

So step, step into the sunshine
of my beauty with you
transcendent prizes of hair
soaked in golden and blue.

Step, step closer,
up onto the stands
microphone in hand
as I lay and listen to your voice,
and wonder at a time like this,
How you are able to speak my name?

The Politics of You:
Acting in Dimensional Alignment
[The Workshop]

a taste…
- seeing yourself out of the corner of your eyes
- unleashing the alchemist through the hands of an artist
- recognizing the purpose in your personal perception
- uncovering the origin of speech, language, & how it affects our thoughts
- listening to subtle sounds
- writing out wrongs
- seeing the you within the universal plot
- recalling the script, playing your part
- turning subtext into psychic activities
- letting go of luggage
- seeing the past as passed aka *the adernochrome theory*
- picking & choosing, precision by releasing limits from potential
- hearing sense in scents
- redefining our history without a need to burn the books
- turning our thoughts into copper, a penny for
- the reality of religion: relative + region
- dancing alongside your parallel partner
- personalizing your impulses, constructing the character [role] of yourself from an impersonal imaginative viewpoint
- hearing your song amongst visions
- broadening the range of sight [colors]

Little Wings / Big Ticket

Forget about the rest,
Forget about the bliss,
The silver, The gold,
Faith held in a necklace.

The face,
The calling,
Forgetting my name.

The laughing,
The eyes,
It all became the same.

The circle keeps spinning,
I keep growing and shrinking.

The doorknob keeps talking—
—and telling me to search.

I keep looking for sunshine
in the roots of the dirt.

I want to,
I crave to,
Feel one with the Earth.

I burn sage in the palo
of my shell-lined hearth.

It's my life!
It's ours!
Laying upon my silver wings.

It's waking,
It's taking
My breathe in a simple string.

So, I write this,
and I feel it running up the stairs,
I'm watching it from beneath favors of secret cares.

So, read this and realize
the selfish wings of devils;
I look at myself
and 1- up my level.

I'm slipping,
I'm dripping
Deep into the Blue.

I'm running and jumping,
I try and reach for the moon.

But my feet have left the cliff,
Oh, what should I do?

"Look deceit in the jaw,
and pray for breakthrough."

Raven

Simple to adornable,
I stand upon a surface
That is something but a word—

Consonants towards contention,
I remark on Rising Raven,
To encircle a past of scorn
is to lift your hands
and cave in.

Symboling towards rafters
of faces left alone,
Becoming one's savior
Upon giving up said
Mind to Stone.

Flinching eyes
Grow on top doors,
Blue becomes disguised
By forces
As silence is unheard.

Loving Eyes

I think about you on days all the regular—
I think thoughts of
"If only I could dish this fish up & make a happy customer,"
Whilst reading seconds of scenes,
Where I pass by in dignity
and whisper last morn'
silent sounds
of sweet serenity.

I dig to be the ground of walking Shaman Healer—
A girl, who can be a child,
and yet, a woman within this commissioned picture.

I care about these things,
When I was like 16,
and got lost like a whale
belly up in a dream.

So I pick up…
… onto the next page,
I scream !!!!

YAWP

Truth filled with unconstitutional damage,
Life, of thee,
I shall be able to manage.
Disguise of the discussed,
"Meeting enemies undaunted,"
We arrive through shipment,
Mouths dripping with words haunted.

Oh! Continue towards the dark!
Why can we make speech
of something forgot?
Agony of the tasteless lark,
Singing a soul-fried remark—

Are we heading forwards,
or losing sight of God?
"Oh, Captain! My Captain!"
—Thinking of sunken thought—
[amongst tender natures of mercy]
no longer do I sweat in shock.

Singular.
Standing South,
I may lose life in laundered locations,
my trough is complete with water,
but I must catch up on sleep filled vacations.

LORD,
Lead me towards empathetic ways
and the disappointment of constituency
within supple trays
that are stacked
with silver confessions
and disregarded forays.

Take my phalanges
and lead me where…
where there cannot be
shifting happiness bought,
but only Holy marriage
of honesty
of thought.

Freedom is there,
Just look—
It is clear,
over the horizon

[Stage Flat]

Whatever It Takes [The Hymn]

Oh, to see what thou
hast restored within—
of yourself,
selfish,
loathing of
your own ways.

I just opened a fortune cookie
with no fortune inside it
… unfortunate?

Sugar Magnolia

It's when you shut your own doors,
Can't seem to stand them anymore!
It's a chance to be alone in your head,
It's really just Being >>
to >> walking Dead.

What do you consider your greatest extravagance?
~~To be unlike anyone else~~
For everyone to be unlike anyone else

What's up with life and stuff?

Fun

What is longing
Yet a way to see
The desperate idea of life on a timeline?
Reconnaissant to reminders
That repeat in verse
On the realm of …

The Stand-in Hotel

We are going to lose our head,
We are going to win!

We are going to breeze past ideals of description!

We are,
We is,
—wee, wee, wee—
go the shining children!

—·—·—·—·—

10/19/14

Pebbles & Marbles,
as if things weren't dust—
My Mind
playing tricks on itself,
leaving myself behind.

Comrade Down

Where did my brain go?
Out to play?
Is it still standing in the shadow of empty stomachs,
Lost in outlandish display?

I lay and wither,
distributed in what is disturbed.
I stand up to be like that movie and deliver,
I hope to get the applause I deserve.

Are hours too long to stand lone,
or do days pass by,
as I loafe on my own…?

Instrumental Breakdown

Linger like swoon :
      Way too soon.
I move on through
      To the morning rise
      To greet the day
With greedy eyes.

Puppet Act

With intentions to help,
I do nothing but kill.
I fill up with air,
and give up my ability to feel.
I forget about reality,
I forget about trust,
I tell you I am sorry,
I am so very sorry,
I have become such a fuss.
I've let go of your hand,
I've come to terms with our bond,
I've forgotten what it is like
to just lay freely on the lawn.
I want to sink my eyes deep into the red,
I want to stay perched forever at the end of your bed.
I want to cut yesterday
and aid it with tomorrow,
I want to stand up
and *stop* the senseless follow,
because around here you stand alone,
if at all!
And once you've reached average,
You're bound to get caught in the Fall.
I've tripped, I've missed, I've lost tract of direction (all ways),
I've hit, I've kissed and held hands with deception.
So read my words back and then forth,
and I'll swallow them whole with a spoon;
I'll be forced to sit by the window
and constantly recall early afternoons.
I've given up!
I've let go!
I've forgot my ambition!
I've set out and decided to fool with correction!
So listen, just once, if you hear me at all,
Don't mess with the sun,
You're locked in a house of dolls.

December 6, 2008

23

I synchronize myself on the plane of all existence.
— — — —

"What does this mean?" The Wind asks The Fly.
"It means that chance is within your realm of chosen ideas, if you choose to believe."
"But that doesn't rhyme…" She replies to The Fly.
The Fly then answers as it drifts on by,
"That is yours to figure out on this beautiful ride."
— — — —

She was living in California, when she lost her mind.
She was living her life, one realization at a time.
She was catching herself up on the book she had already written,
yet she didn't quite understand the idea of liquid time being smitten.

She was living in California, when she found herself,
dreaming about a person that lives on her shelf,
a person that is everywhere and led her to develop,
a person that loves everything and herself.

She was living in California, one poem at a time.
She was living in California on pattern and rhyme.
She was watching the days, as she met herself,
one moment,
dancing with another
to create feelings felt.

The Dozing Dozen
~~Contemplation~~

So much air
does the vac take
to be around in life
with the being of essence
in hand
Alice is no idea of demands
reminding of
thus bars its time
to farm the growth
and be of oath
to squire redundant round arrows —
stow it away!
I see
I am blind
and quite transcendent
in the droplet
of precipitation
perfection is such
as this
resounding an idea
of a tactic.

WAILING AFTERNOON

Be the bunny & the hat! Be the eye & the contact!

With smiles amidst Joy,

The Moon reigns down tears of recognition,

and messages written in undetectable noise.

Sounds to gaze and see past,

A day dependent on haze.

I recount the communal blessings,

in infinite, countless ways.

Honoring My Grandfather, Milton Ralston Brown

In Gratefulness, I thankfully believe—
that all is now, manifesting—

and from your soul,

I discovered thyself in me,
and I took to heart the Art of living…
When I take a Breath, I, now, recede——

to the initial barriers that determine the farm from the country.

To be of fruit that grows from Truth's vine,
To be of root that resounds throughout time—

For, in your eyes, I witnessed the portal of thy Soul;
I saw the within—
forsaking my necessity for control.

In the wake,

I rise from my stone of gold:

brushing off such shoulders,

that we were told to grow old.

I tell myself in seconds,

of minutes in rhyme,

to allow my best intentions to surface,

naturally, sourcing Kind.

I was running with the bridges,

I thought to burn and meld;

I was vicariously living through

the Milton I felt.

We Are Farmers
[A Dedication to The Browns]

The initial power to give
is the incentive to breathe.
The bravery to admit
is the will to succeed.

I see gift amongst doubt,
due to short stacks,
I see, I can do
and overcome all I lack—

Because of you,
and because of thee;
I see straight through veils
and discriminating
factors
attempting to hold true,
but who is who?

I find myself
along tales or fates
I already knew—
to and through—
Onward! We press,
because tomorrow is welcome,
and negativity can only result in distress!

I am wholesome!
I am whole!
I am,
because of you!
I can see,
I can feel
the veil,
I pierce through!

A totem of sorts,
I total my goal.
I craft myself out of marble;
well, you already know—
You are all,
and I am—
Me,
because you allow,
I can see!

I thank you for providing my eyes,
when once blind.
I am ambitious,
I am Scottish,
I am one of a kind—
I am Brown,
I am Black,
I am the Grayscale to White,
I am,
I am
The one who can carry the light.

I thank you for blessing me
with the ability to retrieve
thoughts beyond my Mindset,
thoughts,
I never thought
I could dream.

You are the backbone,
that holds up mine face,
You are the one who is always there
to wipe up my tears
with grace.
I love,
I receive,
I give,
I leave;
I am able,
I am new,
I am the You within You.

League of Legends

EXT. VENICE BEACH, DAYTIME.

FADE IN:
CENTER is walking on the shoreline of the beach with SPEAKER, both are bundled up in a mixture of layered sweaters with rolled up pants or shorts on the bottom. They are walking barefoot. It is misty outside, where the weather looks like it's morning throughout the whole day. We get the sense that it may be wintertime. We can tell CENTER is somewhat familiar with the area, and SPEAKER is following her lead.

CENTER
(Remembering) The day was a grassy one.
I can definitely remember the tone was cheery.
The type of sunny day, where the sky is just straight blue— where it's so entirely blue and so entirely beautiful that a part of you wants to paint a few clouds in there, and so you do… or I do, or we do. (pause)

CUT TO:
A vague memory starts to be revealed, fading in from the previous shot, we see a photograph take form from CENTER's recollection being discussed. We see the outline of two individuals. We cannot quite make out who the picture is of, because the recollection is hazy. Before we can see any distinct facial features or distinguishing details in the picture of a memory, we cut back to the two characters, CENTER and SPEAKER walking on the beach. This happens because CENTER snaps out of concentrating, and we happened to be viewing this memory from her perspective.

CUT BACK TO: EXT. VENICE BEACH, DAYTIME.

CENTER (cont'd).
… Sorry, I —

SPEAKER
Can I offer you something?

CENTER
Yes.

SPEAKER
Stop being sorry for who you are.
That is no way to live.
In-fact, how are you supposed to live if you are not living as yourself?
If you were not yourself, then you, yourself, would not be.

CENTER
How do you always know what to say? ...
It's like you're reading from a script, and I'm just fumbling around like a ducking idiot... Quacking about things... A bunch of things...
Things that really matter to me though...

SPEAKER
So, keep telling me your story.

CENTER
Right! The day in the field—

CUT TO:
EXT. DRUGSTORE/CVS PARKING LOT, DAYTIME.

We meet CENTER outside CVS Pharmacy on the corner of Rose Ave. and Main St. in Venice Beach, CA. She is holding the photograph of her and TRAVELER taken during their day in the field. This was described as a memory in the previous scene. CENTER has just picked up this roll of developed film from the drugstore, hence why she is standing outside looking at how the picture turned out. The photograph of her memory in the grassy field has not turned out well; however, we can see the photograph clearer than in the previous scene, because CENTER is taking her time to focus in on this memory. In the photo, we see two individuals lounging on the grass. CENTER is sitting on the left, writing in a notebook, and a man is sitting on her right, holding a guitar. However, we cannot see who the man is, because the top right corner of the photograph has turned white due to overexposure, leaving his identity up to the imagination. CENTER then looks up from the photograph to reveal TRAVELER standing across from her. Love in his eyes. We get a sense that the TRAVELER pictured in the photo is a different TRAVELER from the one standing in front of her, yet they also eerily give off the same vibe, as if one is the other's alter-ego.

TRAVELER
If I may be so blessed as to see the masterpiece.

CENTER
It didn't turn out like I thought it would.

CENTER looks back down at the photograph for a split second before handing it to TRAVELER. When she looks back up to hand it to him, he is suddenly gone. She feels saddened by his disappearance.

CUT TO:
EXT. VENICE BEACH, DAYTIME.

We return to CENTER and SPEAKER on the shoreline of the beach. CENTER has just recalled this memory of being with TRAVELER, about to show him the picture of her life when he disappears. We see her confusion mixed with disappointment. Both enjoying their walk soaked in emotion, CENTER and SPEAKER are close enough to the ocean that their toes are touching the water's tide. She stops walking in inquisitive contemplation. She turns to SPEAKER with urgency in her voice and in her eyes.

CENTER
Do you ever wonder where the fuck you are—

SPEAKER
On the beach.

CENTER
—and then wonder where the fuck another person is?

SPEAKER
A person or a soul?

CENTER
Right… So—

She then snaps back to continuing to describe the story of her memory of the grassy, sunny day in the field, the same memory as in her photograph.

CENTER
It was a sunny day. One of those days, where even the morning time is filled with clarity. It was one of those rarer than world-peace moments, at least for me… See, I'm no morning glory… I am not one of those "Ooooooh, rise and shine", "woop-de-fucking-doo", "smell the coffee, YEAH!" type of people. I'm more like… a roll-over, and press le snooze button multiple times in a row type person.

SPEAKER
Right.

CENTER
But for some reason, this particular morning, I open my eyes, and it was like boom! A spark of lightning came over me, and I am up on my feet! I am excited for the day, and I feel no weight of the external world on my shoulders. I felt moved to move for the first time. It was the strangest feeling for me, because… it sounds so stupid… but for the first time in a while, I was drawn to move, simple as that. (pause)

CENTER looks out over the vast ocean, taking in her size in comparison. She sees a sail boat out in the distance. She carries on with her story.

CENTER
At the time, I lived tucked behind this canyon area about five-ish miles up from the beach in the mountains of Malibu, a bit North of here, and… yeah, most of the time I took those mountains for granted. I used to feel so guilty. I… I… I still do, actually, because I lived in such a beautiful, explorable area, and I did nothing. I let fear (*stops*, sighs)… whatever.

CENTER stops speaking. She allows fear into her thought of speaking. She no longer wants to share her story from this special day. She acts like she forgets the details so she doesn't have to finish telling SPEAKER the story about her experience with TRAVELER.

SPEAKER
Is something the matter?

CENTER
(Closes self off from SPEAKER)
Well, the story is actually mostly a daydream, so… I… you know, kind of forget bits and pieces… and I mean… I don't want to tell you a story that's half a dream anyways. It's not realistic. I mean it's practically a lie. Like yes, that day… I did end up adventuring in the canyons and mountains for a bit, and I discovered much lyrical poetry of my soul's self, but the rest is a daydream. The main part of the story is all totally in my head.

SPEAKER
It all is.

CENTER puts her right hand on her heart, recalling how real this daydream felt to her innocent, young soul. She enters a meditative state, deciding to redirect her focus. We experience a schism or break in her personality as her intention moves inward to self.

CUT TO:
HALL OF MEMORIES, CENTER'S MEMORIES.

Shot changes: Via her left eye, the audience enters her mind, experiencing the transition from CENTER talking on the beach — to seeing inside CENTER's head. We see her memories in a hallway format. It is her library of memories. This collection takes the shape of a panorama-type view. Imagine a giant wall of televisions projecting every moment of her memories in every direction of her experience.

CENTER decides to change her focus onto a different memory than her conversation with SPEAKER about TRAVELER. We zoom in on a frame with vibrant colors, as she selects another memory to focus on. We start to experience this other memory with her as we overhear:

CENTER (Voice-Over)
Oooh, this one looks like fun!

The camera pans over, revealing a previously unseen facet of her mind as we realize that this memory comes from her future. The scene brings us to her, one and a half years later, sitting in her new apartment in Denver, Colorado, typing up this script on her laptop... Moments earlier, she had just decided that she did not want to elaborate anymore on the grassy, sunny day field memory shared with TRAVELER, so she begins writing about this current moment. She is in time with herself experiencing it. She begins typing up **this exact sentence. She then pauses, as she realizes she is within a dimensional loop. She finally understands that she is both the writer of her own script and the force feeding it.** *Via an over-the-shoulder shot, we see her writing <u>this</u>. The cursor on her document is blinking, asking her to write more... | | | | | | | |*

CENTER then hears an echo of her own voice coming from within the room. She swivels in her chair trying to figure out where the voice is coming from. When she turns to look behind her, she sees her own ghost standing there, about ten feet away, and THE GHOST whispers in her ear...

THE GHOST
Trippy, right?

SCENE

NOT 1% SURE
Only a fool throws
their own
pity party.

R. S. V. P.

SOULY NOW

The breath of my fire is doused in the clarity of your reigning truth >>
I fill my booth with kisses,
that echo divinity forth,
from mouths of sweet
and knowingly undermined conditions containing youth—

Howling at the projection,
of the Grand Gemini New Moon,
I melt into my Highest Self,
bringing fruition into my being,
and unleashing the will of my soul to bloom.

A season of success,
remains a seasonal dish of choice,
that I positively recycle,
and cyclically ignite by expressing
my beauty filled voice—

The echo of my shadows,
was unveiled at the root
to be patterns:
A temple of my heart,
directed mindfully by the motive of my actions—

Forming from the source of tranquility,
my intention provides the matches >>
I use continuously,
~ to remind my body of its passions ~

~ I dance ~ I sing ~

— I act with all thankfulness —

•}}I dedicate my existence to my highest greatness{{•

Words from Mother

My honest opinion about
Houston, Denver, and LA is…
it's a bottomless pit
of shit you can write about.

Words from Father
No writer likes a deadline.

Words from Self
You can do this.
[Alive with the sound of music].

A SERIES OF SELF: KENDRA, PT. V

The motion of joy is the choreographer of my soul.
Once open to arriving,

I had no need to visualize a door.
For, like the butter,

I could not believe

that I was the Homeowner

and also, the Key.
Oh! How foolish it would be!

To be matter of fact!

To be like a deck of cards,

and keep my choices down to a neat, even stack!

I would rather an art of attention,

than an art made for stakes—

To pile them up,

and buy a way to escape.
I need not a thing.

Therefore, I accept,

all that I am,

and all I attract.
Daily are reminders

sent to me,

by Messenger Birds,

who sing of the Trees.
I see the way

is to untether my soul,

and feather my wings

with the dawn light of gold.
Nestled like light

in the valleys of prosperity,

I set forth the gift of MagicK,

and cyclically receive.
I offer my voice,

from the Knowledge I hold–

We discuss the course of action

is to let the Be of Now unfold.
I offer a dance

to the spirit of me.

I waltz with the waking,

and jive with the free.
Igniting every Moment,

and moving like a scene,

the power of intention

is the Head we feed.
I prance to the beat

of the sound I Believe;

I humm and return

the chant, as I sing!
I wail on the chords,

echoing My Heart

in Harmony, as I create

my own ethos

and walk the path

of Lady Liberty!
The essence of life

is born within the entity

that assumes no barrier
between Now and eternity.

n e w m o o n   in Virgo

I focus my intentions on manifesting destiny.
I remember, I remember - -
What clarity my eyes can see;
I am fruitful in my efforts,
and forgive all happening of thee.

I put efforts towards the sunny mountainous goals—
from flow through all
My spirit of music sent through
My soul.

I listen strongly to my heart;
Confidence in that
that trots through the Wood
of said hill of a mind
of which made to do good.

I love unconditionally all that is all.
I see rays of sunshine float
through all
my fellow blithe human eyeballs!

I am alive - -
I remember what to do.
I am confident. I am brave;
I remember to follow through.

Like the guidance of my own,
I am joyful in my actions that convey
I am alone to the bone.
I am invisible to thought's core.
I am strong among cells of abundance
that Hydrate and Cure.
I radiate with blissfilled energy.
I am Rainbow.
I remember.
I can see; I am free.

I am concentration.

I am; I am.
I am cleansed of all past.
I delete the past tense
and create a path
only I have ever known.

For see,
I heal.
I banish all meanlessness.
I am awake; I answer the call.
I walk through walls,
as I am invisible to all.

On dimensional commandings,
I make my decision
allowing space
the form of precision.

A viewable library
is within,
I move to Colorado;
I am Joy in Action !!

[8/31/16]

BUFFALO WALK
"To be a rock and not to roll…"

Buffalo Walk in the walk of the chant right by,

is of voice,

Rings truth divine.

Of seeding,
Of sowing,

Of being right here,

Of joining the crowd

For the knowledge so dear.

I love the beat of the slant in my talk

When I am the wind

And you the tall grass.

Go and find every moment,

Your sound is the meadow

That circles round the space

Of jams,

To float in the cloud

of, of, of…

Oh, to be the lightning bolt,

Riding on the sea!

Oh, to be the determinous volume

of sounds reverberating!

To be, to be, to be alive!

About a melody

That is the jive!

To groove, to groove, to groove on by!

Round the rhythm

Of inspiration—

Inspiration divine!

Smiles in, Smiles out,

Miles and miles—

Oh, Joy about!!

Do people laugh at me

or all around?

How does one differentiate sound?

To throw one of course,

Only to fool.

To act, to act, to act so cool.

To freeze, To burn, To live it off,

To be the sun,

That has a cough,

To be the magnet that holds the sloth—

In the room til it forgot.

Then brought it back to be a scene,

To trick a trickster,

Good luck.

That's obscene—

Peace and prance,

and love on by,

Be the wind that leads the fly.

Choose the words

To be your grace—

"Choose the good,"

Chants the human race.

SEAL OF THE LEAGUE

acknowledgements

This book developed from writings I have collected over the past 10 years, though these memories last on and on and on. I thank the english teacher I had freshman year of high school, Liz McIlravy, for introducing me to this art form. Many of those originals poems have remained and transformed. You can see them gracing these thick pages. I am eternally grateful for all the moments that reverberate through my life. I am grateful for the family that co-created this with me. We all know their names.

These poems, these lyrics, they have depth, real depth. They can't die. They can't be decoded, inextinguishable. It began summertime of 2015. I realized I was living in my work. I believe the film, *My Dinner with Andre,* said it best when quoting Ingrid Bergman in *Autumn Sonata,*
"I could always live in my art, but never in my life."

- — — — -

It may haunt me to know
that people can read me,
but it will definitely haunt me to know,
I didn't try and be heard.

- — — — -

The fragments of my life have been poured into this book,
one shot at a time.
You may recognize some of the characters I discuss.
They have changed over time, yet always remain.
One person turned to another,
who turned to another,
who spoke to me
in dreams.

I urge you to take these words as offerings to the source, to the Earth, to the people, to the soul. You are with me, and I am thankful.

Thank you for reading me.

Ultimately, this is the politics of you.

To close, I ask you chant this aloud,
"I am sound."

A Special Thank You to all the musicians, those who pave the way.

New Age Wasteland, photo by Mary Frances Looke, Mulberry Park, pg. 23.
Fluffy Bell-Bottoms, Major Arcana XIII: Death (2014), painting by Ericka Frost, pg. 31.
Let There Be Words, Seal of The League, seal accredited to Timothy Leary, *Turn on, Tune In, Drop Out,* pg. 33.
Watch Yourself, Learning; photo by Beth Muecke, styled by Bethie Life, Cosmo and Nathalia's Glam Squad, pg. 38.
Parliamentary, Watson; photo by Harmonic Light [Reid Godshaw], Purple 33, pg. 39.
The White Board, photo with Matthew Sells, Museum in Santa Fe, NM, pg. 42.
Sweet Orange, Deep Blue; photo by Amy Brlansky, Albuquerque High School, ISAS 2011, pg. 43.
Inspiration is the Theme of a Place; inspired by Occidental Bar, Denver, CO, pg. 75.
New Wage Caseland, mention of song "The Rabble" by Sound Tribe Sector 9, pg. 60.
The New Somatic, inspired by Sound Tribe Sector 9's documentary, *#ReGeneration*, pg. 77.
Totemed Up Freestyle, photo by Beth Muecke, styled by Bethie Life, pg. 81.
Words from Brother, inspired by Harrison Muecke, pg. 90.
Portal-able, photo by Travis Shivers, Spring Frequency Music Festival, La Jolla, CA, pg. 92.
Perspectivity: The Parable of The Queen & The Sad One, photo of Beth Muecke, Linda Porter. National Academy of Dance, Champagne, IL, pg. 94.
Words from Sister, inspired by Ayla Nereo, the sistersoul, pg. 97.
Words from Friend, inspired by Jaquel Andrews, pg. 112.
Oh, Tweeze! inspired by Phish, pg. 114.
Welcome, This is A Wheelhouse, inspired by The Waterwheel Foundation, The Mockingbird Foundation, Phish. Madison Square Garden, pg. 119.
Seven Sisters, One Pact. inspired by the witchcraft family and the sistersoul, pg. 122.
Ode To Dancer, photo of and inspired by Beth Muecke in-front of Edgar Degas painting, styled by Bethie Life, pg. 123.
Words from Chief, inspired by Sound Tribe Sector 9, pg. 128.
Something Over Nothing: The Teenage Years, photo by Mary Ann Cuellar, Austin City Limits Music Festival 2008, pg. 134.
Degrade A Beef, Calabasas, CA, pg. 141.
Lying to Yourself: For Dummies, quote at bottom from *It's Always Sunny in Philadelphia,* pg. 142.
The Song, photo ft. Toblerone the Fluffbunny, Stevie Windwood the guitar. Venice Beach, CA, pg. 143.
A Thinking Place, inspired by Sancho's Broken Arrow, Denver, CO; pg. 146.
A Series of Self: Kendra, pt. I; Hermann Park, Houston, TX; pg. 152.
Processing The Negatives, photo by Kendra Muecke, Hermann Park, Houston, TX; pg. 153.
Whilst in The Fiction of Skeletal Measures: Sonnet I, inspired by "Sonnet 106: When in the Chronicle of Wasted Time" by William Shakespeare, photo of Mary Frances Looke, pg. 154.
Dead Fish, photo by Mary Frances Looke, pg. 156.
Will, Son!, photo editing by Kendra Muecke, pg. 157.
Summer, photo of Nicole Lazarz, pg. 164.
Butterflys* With Bandages, photo of Alisa Fedele, Heaps n Heaps band. Los Angeles, CA; title of poem inspired by Vivian Wise, pg. 165.

The Butterfly Effect, photo by Mark Matcho, Lightning in A Bottle Music Festival 2016, pg. 172.
What'd You Find, inspired by Jumpsuit Records, pg. 178.
The Portrait, inspired by Seinfeld; season 7, episode 11, pg. 179.
The Companion; inspired by The Prairie Home Companion ft. Ernest Anastasio, Ellie Caulkins Opera House, Denver, 2016.
Karmic Names, photo by Beth Muecke, styled by Bethie Life, Houston SPCA, pg. 194.
Channel 11, Parallel News; photo of Ganesha, styled by Katie Tyler, Los Angeles, CA, pg. 195.
Share Your Shoes, photo of Shadow Self, Venice Beach, CA, pg. 204.
Reservation(s): Lightning in A Bottle Music Festival 2016, pg. 206.
The Pulley, quote from Waking Life by Richard Linklater, pg. 208.
Illuminine (9), Not Undermine; quote featured by David Foster Wallace, Sancho's Broken Arrow, Denver, CO, pg. 215.
The Lullaby of Lady Liberty, nyc. inspired by prompt on fear via workshop *Writing our Voices*, lead by Deonte Osayande, National Poetry Slam, Denver, CO, 2017; content of poem inspired by experience at The Baker's Dozen, Phish, MSG, NYC, July 2017; pg. 220.
The Formular, inspired by Karin Dremel via the workshop, *Undoing Writer's Block: Engaging Your Ancestors to Free Your Creative Expression*, National Poetry Slam, Denver, CO, 2017; pg. 221.
Johnny Boy, inspired by Johnny Gohringer, "Shine on You Crazy Diamond" by Pink Floyd, pg. 222.
Around The Bodhi Tree, Verses of A Mirror; self-portrait of Kendra Muecke, Calabasas, CA, pg. 225.
Ж, photo of Kendra Muecke, by Bryan Muecke, Houston, TX; pg. 227.
Trill, inspired by Screwed Up Click, Swishahouse; pg. 240.
Ekphrastic, inspired by painting PH 435; 1935, by Clyfford Still via *Ekphrastic Workshop with Lighthouse Writers*, National Poetry Slam, Denver, CO, 2017; pg. 244.
Ekphrastic, II. inspired by painting PH 247, 1951, Clyfford Still via *Ekphrastic Workshop with Lighthouse Writers*, National Poetry Slam, Denver, CO, 2017; pg. 245.
Ekphrastic, III. inspired by painting PH 1074, 1956 - 59, by Clyfford Still via *Ekphrastic Workshop with Lighthouse Writers*, National Poetry Slam, Denver, CO, 2017; pg. 246.
33333, inspired by Shane Shanley, pg. 247.
New Age Wasteland: Papa... oh, really? inspired by The Who, pg. 257.
Mac & Wood, inspired by Fleetwood Mac, Stevie Nicks, pg. 257.
Copper Gold, Venice Beach, CA, pg. 258.
Next-pionage, Venice Beach, CA, pg. 260.
Magna Carta, inspired by Venice Beach, CA; pg. 261.
The City for Miles, inspired by Denver, CO; pg. 262.
A Peaceful Treaty, Halloween as a young hippie, photo by Beth Muecke, pg. 263.
Whoooo Are You?, Alice and The White Rabbit, by Grace Slick, Be On Key Psychedelic Ripple, Denver, CO, pg. 278.
Phantom, pt. III, inspired by JT Skilling, Syd Barrett, Bruce Hampton, pg. 281.
Moontribe, inspired by the family, moon, spirit, gathering, Moontribe, pg. 284.
The Politics of You: Acting in Dimensional Alignment, inspired by workshop created and curated by Kendra Muecke, pg. 291.
YAWP, inspired by film, Dead Poets Society, pg. 296.
Sugar Magnolia, inspired by the Grateful Dead, pg. 298.
The Stand-in Hotel, inspired by Stanley Kubrick, The Shining. pg. 299.
Wailing Afternoon, art by Find Art Magazine, Lightning in A Bottle Music Festival 2016, pg. 303.

Milton Ralston Brown [Grandfather Mountain], photo of Beth Muecke, Milton Ralston Brown, Rockford, IL, pg. 305.
We Are Farmers [A Dedication to The Browns], inspired by Scottish Heritage, The Browns. pg. 307.
League of Legends, inspired by time traveling, pg. 309.
Words from Mother, inspired by Beth Muecke, pg. 316.
Words from Father, inspired by Bryan Muecke, pg. 317.
A Series of Self: Kendra, pt. V; photo of Shiva as Nataraja, Houston Museum of Fine Arts, pg. 319.
Buffalo Walk, photo by Beth Muecke, styled by Bethie Life, Cosmo and Nathalia's Glam Squad, Los Angeles, CA; quote from "Stairway to Heaven" by Led Zeppelin, pg. 324. Seal of The League, seal accredited to Timothy Leary, *Turn on, Tune In, Drop Out,* pg. 327.
The Politics of You: Acting in Dimensional Alignment, workshop created and led by Kendra Muecke, photo by Alisa Fedele, pg. 334.

Cover art, inspired by *The Catcher in The Rye* by J. D. Salinger.
Back cover, Headshot by Bjoern Kommerell. Seal of The League accredited to Timothy Leary: *Turn On, Tune In, Drop Out.*
Poems featured: *¿Dónde Está Mí Cabeza?, Timeless; Around The Bodhi Tree, Verses of a Mirror.*

thank you...

The Politics of You: Acting in Dimensional Alignment
a workshop on improvisational acting, free-flow writing, and self-spiritualization
Spring Frequency Music Festival 2016
The Healing Temple
La Jolla, CA

about-the-author

Kendra Elisabeth Muecke was born on February 11, 1993 in Houston, TX. Born a true Aquarian, Kendra has always been connected to her creativity and visions, drawing her to the performing arts at a very young age. Starting at 4 years old, Kendra began professional theatrical training at Theatre Under The Stars located in Houston. Attending acting classes, vocal lessons, and dance rehearsals, she found herself in love with the artistic endeavor that is the stage.

Growing up in the theatre, Kendra's voice grew along with her experience. At age 13, she began singing rock 'n roll music at Camp Jam in Houston.
Today, she is a lyricist with a growing affection for the guitar.

At age 14, Kendra discovered her affinity for poetry. Her stream of consciousness prose was noticed immediately by school teachers and mentors alike. At age 15, she was requested to read her long form poem, *October*, in front of her entire high school. The poem and others of hers were additionally published for 4 consecutive years in the literary magazine, *Light and Shadow*. As a poet, her style comes in all forms. From metered to rhythmatic to traditional Shakespearean sonnet, she keeps her pencil in hand and her eyes open for observation. Today, she has expanded into the fields of journalism, live music reviews, fiction and non-fiction essays, screenwriting, playwriting, and stand-up comedy.

At age 18 (2011), She moved to Malibu, CA to attend Pepperdine University. There she continued her studies in the theatre and on stage. Developing her interest in the ancient history of the theatre and its culture, she began studying ritual performance and sacred texts. After graduating from Pepperdine in May 2015 with a Bachelor of Fine Arts in Theatre Arts (Acting), Kendra moved to Venice Beach, CA, where her interest in ritual performance and her affinity for poetry drew her to the path of Shamanism.

She began work as a healer the Summer of 2015, giving her a new perspective on what it means to be a performance artist within the bounds of psychic discovery. Bringing her collective talents together, she created the workshop, *The Politics of You: Acting in Dimensional Alignment*. This workshop based in the realm of spirituality, improvisational acting, and psychic intuitive development was first shared with her community via The Healing Temple at Spring Frequency Music Festival in June 2016, located in La Jolla, CA. Additionally, she performed this workshop at Sonic Bloom Music Festival in June 2017, located at Hummingbird Ranch, CO.

In September of 2016, Kendra packed up her car and headed East from Los Angeles to the Land of Poets, known to many as Denver, CO. Here, she has her feet on the ground and her head in the mountains, as she pursues her next great artistic venture. She is currently working on her first musical album, *"of Vinyl"*. Stay tuned for her 2nd book, *"Project Non-Arch [Operation: Clown School]"* to be released soon!

Sending her words in codes of love, energy, grace, and peace,
she thanks you for all the support.

Her self-published works can be found at **www.thepoliticsofkendra.com**

til next time !!

peace & love,
Kendra

white buffalo calf woman

www.ingramcontent.com/pod-product-compliance
Lightning Source LLC
Chambersburg PA
CBHW081104080526
44587CB00021B/3442